# THE VIOLENT SOCIETY

# THE
# VIOLENT
# SOCIETY

Edited by
ERIC MOONMAN

Foreword by
LORD SCARMAN

FRANK CASS

*First published 1987 in Great Britain by*
FRANK CASS & CO. LTD.
Gainsborough House, Gainsborough Road
London E11 1RS, England

*and in the United States of America by*
FRANK CASS & CO. LTD.
c/o Biblio Distribution Centre
81 Adams Drive, P.O. Box 327, Totawa, N.J. 07511


Copyright © 1987 Frank Cass & Co. Ltd.

British Library Cataloguing in Publication Data

The violent society.
1. Violence
I. Moonman, Eric
303.6'2      HM281


ISBN 0-7146-3309-7
ISBN 0-7146-4055-7 Pbk


Library of Congress Cataloging in Publication Data

The Violent society.

1. Violence.   I. Moonman, Eric.
HM291.V56 1987      303.6'2      86-26833
ISBN 0-7146-3309-7

*Printed and bound in Great Britain by*
*A. Wheaton & Co. Ltd, Exeter*

# CONTENTS

# FOREWORD

Each chapter of this work is in truth a separate essay or article in which an author distinguished in his field treats a different aspect or manifestation of violence in human society. I doubt whether so complete a treatise in so short a compass has been previously attempted.

The reader will be left in no doubt when he reflects on what he has read that violence is, and always has been, a feature or a threat in human society – and will remain so.

The reason why this must be so is made plain in the early chapters. Violent behaviour is a display of man's aggressive instinct: without that instinct, which he (and she) shares with the rest of the animal kingdom, the human species would not survive.

On another level of debate it is also essential that a serious review should take place of the relationship between contemporary media and violence and this is to be found in the first chapter.

The challenge, therefore, to civilized mankind is not the elimination of violence but its control and restraint. And the lesson for a civilized society is that unless fear of attack, of deprivation, of frustration, is eliminated within a society the risk of violent outburst by those who see themselves as victims will be greatly enhanced. The problem is more than of maintaining 'law and order': it is also one of achieving a just society.

I have said enough to indicate that the subject of this anthology, though united in a single theme, is complex indeed. I cannot do better than invite you to read from cover to cover this challenging, exciting and sobering work.

*Lord Scarman*

# CHAPTER ONE

# VIOLENCE: MYTHS AND REALITY

## Eric Moonman

Television and the other modern media have fulfilled a very positive function over the last decade or two in making more people aware of the wider world in which they live. News reporting of crises, from earthquakes to terrorist acts, may be witnessed on television within hours or even as they occur. The consequences of this presentation of world news as it is made is that images of violence are disseminated constantly and indiscriminately.

One aspect of violence, namely terrorism provides a vivid example of the negative effects of this phenomenon. Fringe groups, fanatics and their exploiters learn from the activities of their equivalents across the world. Defiance of the law and confrontation become commonplace – a necessary part of extremist politics.

Assassinations, hijackings and riots have all taken place on television before an audience of millions. The issues become obscured by the sheer drama of the events being played out; frequency breeds contempt or, at the very least, indifference. Hijackings are still sufficiently rare to attract huge ratings; overturned cars, stone throwing and burning cars have become so familiar as to be boring. It is an appalling comment on contemporary society that matters which should revolt the consciousness have become models for the criminal, the terrorist and the desperate judged in terms of their entertainment value by the general public.

There is obviously a relationship between terrorism, small-scale war waged by bands of undisciplined recruits on civilian targets and regular wars between nation states fought with sophisticated and devastating weapons. Vietnam was the first

war to be televised though it was not until the 1982 war in
Lebanon that modern technology brought a war into our living
rooms as it was happening. There is no question that this new
dimension to warfare heightens international tension and stimu-
lates the political debate surrounding any conflict. There are
many ways in which this is 'a good thing' but we should not blind
ourselves to the dangers of the greater involvement of huge
numbers of people through mass communications in international conflict. Violence is seen to be a necessary part of
survival from the level of the local neighbourhood to the world
arena. Neither should we ignore the enormous responsibility the
whole phenomenon places on the media. Television cannot yet
decide who wins a war but it can already decide who we *think* is
winning.

On the other hand, consider the iniquities of the exclusion of
the mass communications element. Look at the Soviet involvement in Afghanistan or the bloody and protracted conflict in the
Gulf. Limited media access has not reduced the bloodshed or the
injustice and has had the effect of producing amnesia among the
general public.

The soviets calculated on a world that would lose 'interest' in
Afghanistan as the opportunities for the media to report were
made virtually impossible. In fact, the reports that were 'allowed'
were usually stories of Soviet military successes or improvised
informal reports from Western cameramen and reporters without Soviet permission. But a violent and brutal action was
committed by a nation and it was, although to a limited extent,
observed.

To the public, then, conditioning in terrorism has taken place
whether by individual groups or superpowers. They have seen
and they may well have experienced personally, some of these
'international' disorders. In the United Kingdom a family on the
mainland will know of the tension and terror experienced directly if they have family or friends living in Northern Ireland.

Along with the conditioning comes the *direct personal*
experience. Whether it is mugging in your neighbourhood; a
burglary of an old age pensioner with precious little to take; a hit-
and-run driver who wrecks a family by killing a father or child. Or
the soccer hooligan who terrorised the streets at Luton (before

the cup tie with Millwall in the Spring of 1985) both before and after the game. It is all seen, felt, personally. No longer is it a detached film on T.V. It is here and now with terrible consequences for families, in which the destroyers have no respect for age or children nor circumstances.

What the chapters in this book will seek to examine is the connection between this type of violence, warfare and terrorism, and whether measures taken to curb or even eradicate the phenomenon in the domestic context will have any effect at the other end of the scale. Does one feed the other?

Is violence an inevitable, even necessary part of human existence? If so, can ways be found of channelling it into constructive as opposed to destructive activity? It turns out that the basic question with which we are concerned centres on the difference between aggression and violence, life-giving energy and death-dealing force. Thus we have moved from the specific to the general, from the pragmatic to the philosophical, an inevitable process if this collection of essays is to throw any light at all on the nature of contemporary violence.

The aim of this book is threefold. First, to examine the past, to assess the various trends and malfunctions which create disorder and violence and, second, to relate this historical perspective to the contemporary scene: is there a greater degree of violence today, and, if so, what form does it take? Third, what can be done to reassure a growing, anxious public as they observe hooligans and brutalities within their neighbourhoods affecting their families and friends as many of our social institutions appear to be breaking down?

Professor Pearson indicates the nature and gives a historical assessment of the subject. He describes the roots of violence, and how and why street violence has troubled successive generations of police and government. Yet it is not only that the scale of violence is greater today, on whatever index we may care to choose, but perhaps, most important, that with the growth of knowledge and self-awareness it had been assumed that a more civilised and rational society would emerge.

The violence and rioting on British streets in the summer of 1981 is a relevant case study. It is totally unlike anything most people in this country had experienced before. Many reasons have been given for this breakdown in law and order in so many cities – economic conditions, unemployment, racial discrimination, for instance – and no doubt all these factors have contributed. But if there is one single influence which, more than any other, dictated the form of action when smouldering frustrations was sparked into violence, my enquiries suggest that it is the copy-cat or halo effect of observing confrontations and rioting such as are to be found in Northern Ireland, that long-running saga of social breakdown in Britain which nightly fills the television screens with violent defiance of authority, with street fighting and neighbourhood strife.

The conditions which may create urban violence are to be found on Merseyside. The frustration of unemployment and its accompanying poverty is exacerbated by thirty years of muddled planning which has left large parts of the district derelict – if not literally, spiritually so. Long before the riots I wrote in *The Times* (30 May 1977) of the over-ambition of the planners and their lack of foresight, of the planning blight which drove out small businesses and pushed down the rate revenue, of the drop in population due to rehousing outside the city, and the consequences in social terms:

> By the time any action was taken to counteract this urban decay, it was too late. The downturn in the economy added large-scale unemployment to Liverpool's problems, and if new industry was going to go anywhere, it would be to the new centres of population, not to areas which had been denuded of a large part of their potential workforce. And in the wake of dereliction came all the social problems of today – poor schools whose replacement was long overdue attracting fewer and fewer good teachers, an ageing population, vandalism and crime.

Stephen Gardiner later (*The Observer*, 2 August 1981) wrote of Liverpool's 'mindless post-war building experiments', of 'towers and slabs looming above an eerie wasteland of unkempt grass that was once countryside', of design showing 'total loss of contact with people ... in acres of grey concrete and black tarmac and in the seemingly arbitrary location of identical blocks'; above all he identified the disappearance of the street as having adverse effects on the life of community, so that there was no continuity with the past, no identity with surroundings.

## THE SIGNIFICANCE AND EXAMPLE OF NORTHERN IRELAND

One way and another, the frustration was certainly there, allied with a sense of alienation from society as a whole and a distrust of the establishment in all its forms; it needed only a spark and an example. The spark came in different ways – an arrest, a fight, it varied from place to place – the example was Northern Ireland. The parallel is not an artificial one. Northern Ireland is part of Britain and many mainland families have relatives there. There is no substantial difference between parts of Liverpool and parts of Belfast, while the emotional differences between Catholic and Protestant exist in some parts of the mainland as they do in the Province, or have their local equivalent. Looking back to the beginning of the current period of Northern Ireland unrest the same factors can be seen at work – high unemployment, regional neglect, a minority discriminated against, a Government which failed to see the problems. But in Northern Ireland the story has been different – for years open warfare has replaced frustration. Arbitrary killing, kidnapping, brutality, and the wholesale destruction of buildings, with as little regard for hospitals and schools as in a conventional war, have become the means for communication; and the frustrations of ordinary decent people have provided a field day for the bully boys, the criminals and the psychopaths.

And as the thugs take over, the rights and wrongs of the situation get lost. Horror and helplessness combine in rejection not only of the violence but also of those whose sufferings are made worse, not lessened, by it. Already we have seen the same response to Brixton, Toxteth and Tottenham; but we must try to understand before it is too late.

For if the destruction practised in Northern Ireland is condemned by most people in Britain, it nevertheless offers something to those whose own sense of alienation and frustration has reached breaking-point. For our access to news today is such that we can see in our own homes the destruction and the killing within minutes of its happening, and sometimes even while it is happening; so that we know not only that it can be done – even here in Britain – but also how it's done.

### ENQUIRIES ON MERSEYSIDE

My enquiries in support of this thesis arise from a series of reports, albeit dealing with football violence, and Fascist recruitment in schools and at rock concerts, undertaken by the Centre of Contemporary Studies, all stressing the seriousness of such action committed against a background of public interest and viewing participation.[1]

Second, and more specifically, on the question of the 1981 summer's riots, I visited a number of the trouble centres where, during interviews, the significance of the copy-cat crime became clear to me from many points of view. As part of this investigation I interviewed youngsters in Toxteth in August, immediately after the riots. The influence of television on their response to the situation could not be doubted – TV made it look easy, they knew what kind of things to do. Aged between 13 and 15, half of them white and half black, bored, brought up to distrust police and, in four cases, with parents away, when the opportunity to riot came, they took it; they weren't scared because such happenings were not 'unthinkable'; they are, indeed, part of the media wallpaper of their everyday lives.

Further enquiries, both in Liverpool and later in South London again, emphasised the significance to this age group of television viewing. One comment from a 16-year-old in South London makes the point:

> I'm out of work. I'm bored with everything around me. To try out for real what I see on the box is good thinking. I've been into all the fights, with the shop windows, the pigs, the lot. It's so bloody easy. That's what's so funny. It's as easy as watching it happen in Ireland.... This is the London show....

Further evidence for the existence of the copy-cat response to media events is well documented, particularly in America where universities have encouraged examination of such questions as part of their long history of media analysis. Links between the media and imitative events have been established in such diverse examples as suicides by Russian roulette following showings of the film *The Deer Hunter*, and a correlation between the monthly suicide rates and front-page coverage of suicides in *The New York Times* taken over a period of 20 years.

The susceptibility of young people in the 10 to 13 age group is particularly high, as a 1978 Harvard and Yale[2] research project demonstrated. This is the age when children begin to move into the adult world and, as the Annan Committee on the Future of Broadcasting[3] pointed out, for the disadvantaged child television is the main source from which he draws his knowledge of how adult society behaves. This factor was clearly recognised in the nationwide outbreak of copy-cat street violence which followed Brixton and Toxteth, but has been overlooked as a factor in Brixton and Toxteth themselves. Yet the similarity to the Northern Ireland scene was remarked on by many commentators without recognising that the similarity was neither superficial nor coincidental. The wearing of balaclavas and plastic bags to conceal identity, the firing of dustbins, the commandeering of milk floats, the petrol bombs, the looting – all this was a clear reflection of the pictures of life in Northern Ireland as we see it on our television screens, torn from the total context of Northern Ireland, in which the majority of people abhor the violence as much as any mainlander and carry on their day to day lives as normally as possible, and where many people work quietly behind the scenes to bring peace and reconciliation. For the response of the media to the copy-cat phenomenon lies not in censorship, but in balance, in putting the news into its proper perspective as the exceptional rather than the norm.

At the mention of any restraint of the broadcasting authorities there are a lot of knee-jerks. 'It smells of censorship', said a trade union leader when I tentatively suggested the matter. But the issue is now being faced as it will not go away. For the first time, in December 1985, the Home Secretary convened a meeting with the heads of the BBC and the Independent Broadcasting Authority to discuss the level of violence shown on television.

The meeting provided the Home Secretary with an opportunity to convey public concern to the two broadcasting chair-

men. Earlier, at a conference of trade unionists in Blackpool, the
Prime Minister had told her audience that 'violence on television
was damaging to young people who watched it night after night.
She said the government was considering what further could be
done.' Her concern was then reinforced in an interview by the
Home Secretary on BBC television. He said the broadcasters
should 'set their house in order' over violence. He went on:
'Concern about this is very real. I think the most emotional
meeting I have had in my constituency in recent years was on this
subject, from parents who came together regardless of party to
hammer away at me, the MP and BBC and ITV representatives.'

It would be desirable for the broadcasting authorities rather
than the government to take measures themselves to reduce the
level of violence on television. At present, commercial television
is under a statutory duty to ensure that programmes do not offend
against good taste and decency or incite crime. Similar obligations are imposed on the BBC under its charter. But the
opponents of any form of restraint on the media argue from
different motives. Political extremists say – whether on the left or
right – that there should be no control of the media, but in reality,
and from experience in other countries, it is clear that they would
not hesitate to use such powers against their opponents if they
were in government.

Opposition to restraint of the media also comes from the
artistic. This is from the talented playright Hanif Kureishi (in *The
Times*, 28 December 1985):

> Since there is already adequate provision to prevent ordi-
> nary people being shocked by unusual or unlikely sex or
> violence, it is increasingly apparent that this renewed call
> for censorship is a figleaf concealing the desire to suppress
> work which is morally or politically challenging. The extent
> to which the authoritarian suppression of dissent – be the
> dissenters trade unions, artists or the BBC – is becoming
> more general in our society now is already worrying enough.
> But this fresh attack is deeply dangerous.
>
> As it is through the imaginative arts that we tell the truth
> to ourselves, writers and directors who seek to explore the
> serious and difficult issues of sex and violence are essential

to any society that considers itself tolerant, sceptical, pluralist and self-aware.

This is not only a question of the freedom of artists, but one about the importance a society attaches to criticism.

Mr Kureishi was answering correspondence on the showing of violence in television serials. But whilst he stressed the 'rights' of artists and writers to express themselves freely he offers no guidance to help an audience to understand, to relate or even to refute what it sees. Besides, it is one thing for writers to intellectualise on the Royal Court stage for a minority few hundred each evening, but it is a very different thing when the message is transmitted on TV to millions of young people, indiscriminately, able to see in their own living room a harrowing series of violent acts. The error in the statements made by Mr. Kureishi and others is that they assume that the same critical faculties and standards are to be found in the millions of people who watch television nightly as in those who form the intellectual groups around Sloane Square.

There are no politicians represented in this book. This is deliberate. I wished to offer ideas and background material on the subject and not slogans. Gerald Kaufman, Labour's shadow home secretary, did little in attempting to find a solution to the issues surrounding the 1985 violence in Britain when he described the government's economic policy as 'their own kind of crime' against our inner city areas. Other politicians have made even more inflammatory speeches on the subject. I suggest that there is no parallel to the violence we have seen in the past five years, and it is a misconception to imagine any serious analysis or answers to be found in such narrow political slogans. The extent to which social and political change may be achieved without recourse to violence is worthy of far greater study than it has received hitherto.[4]

A number of suggestions are made by the authors here, and the immediate concern of the church (described by the Rev. Marcus Braybrooke) offers promise and opportunity. At the same time, the public needs reassurance from politicians of all parties. Perhaps a start might be made, for instance if there was to be a joint declaration on the need to ensure justice for the victims of violent crime. The criminal justice system has never had much interest in victims as such. It judges and punishes offenders not for the sake of individuals but to satisfy society. Meanwhile contemporary culture has focused on offenders, their 'rights', their capacity for rehabilitation. All perfectly understandable within the standards and expectations of contemporary society. But for victims there is no network of help, and it comes hard to people, and to their family and friends, when the circumstances of violence are known.

It looks to the public as if contemporary culture has focused, somewhat excessively, on offenders and their 'rights'. For victims of violence there is no agency support and no financial aid from the State beyond the scale rates of the Compensation Board. But now the victim and his or her needs must be heard. In 1985, the Government decided in a white paper to make it easier to claim compensation. One example is that the police would advise victims of their rights before the board.

Women and children form two particularly vulnerable groups in contemporary society. The abuse of women and children and the scale of violence against them both in the home and in the street cannot be entirely explained by undertaking a general review of violence in society. In particular, there are specific crimes directed against women which require separate analysis and interpretation. The battered wives syndrome was first brought to contemporary prominence by Erin Pizzey who established Women's Aid and a much publicised refuge in Chiswick. Well in advance of state and local government interest, Mrs. Pizzey saw the need to provide shelter, comfort and advice to women and children who were the victims of domestic violence, and the equally urgent necessity for counselling for the man who committed the violence. Mrs. Pizzey began to build up a profile of the families involved in regular and consistent domestic violence, and this has been taken a stage further by the detailed records kept by staff and lay officers of the Basildon Emergency Accommodation Project described in this volume by Jane Moonman, one of the project's trustees. By encouraging women who sought refuge at the Basildon Project to tell their own stories and to answer up to 70 questions about their own and their partners' backgrounds, she has been able to reach tentative conclusions

about the kind of men who beat their families and the kind of women who tend to be their victims.

People turn to the law when they see disruption and chaos in their neighbourhood. The immediate reaction to the events at Tottenham and Birmingham in 1985 was an increased demand for police help and protection. Despite all the agitation and campaigning from the political extremists, whose platforms inevitably challenge existing law and order, the majority of ordinary men and women need the framework they provide to exist happily in society. Richard Clutterbuck examines whether the law is adequate to deal with the scale of violence today. He also looks at the proposition that the law is too slow to cope with today's level of social and political demands.

Terrorism is a form of violence which extends beyond national boundaries. Professor Paul Wilkinson has been concerned with research into this area for a number of years and he has long argued that, while terrorists usually insist that they are not criminals, many of their activities are of purely criminal intent, and more evidence is emerging of a close similarity between the methods and activities of organised crime and those of terrorist groups such as the IRA and the PLO. The application of the rule of law and the strategy of criminalisation lies at the heart of the West's attempts to control terrorism. In response, most terrorist groups seek a special status, claiming that they are not criminals but politically motivated 'freedom-fighters'. A *Guardian* leader on 4 April 1986 raised a fundamental question for those who have to deal with international terrorism. It expressed the view that we should come to terms with terrorism in this way: 'It is better to recognise what you can't control ... far better to treat terrorism as a pathological condition. Take the most stringent prophylactic measures that come to hand, but recognise that it cannot be conquered.' That cannot be a satisfactory response to the need to protect people and institutions in contemporary society. It is not particularly consistent with the newspaper's views on other matters such as racism, fascism or even AIDS. Terrorism needs a treatment and a cure, as Paul Wilkinson describes in his chapter.

This volume treats the issues of contemporary violence with a fairly broad brush. It is the intention of the Centre for Contemporary Studies to identify the *relationship* between the different kinds of violence we face and their shared characteristics.

Can we learn anything from this juxtaposition? Can we offer anything to the politicians on which they can base legislation or action? Perhaps some still need convincing that we live in a violent society. Perhaps this book will persuade them that there is a link between unemployment and violence, between poverty and violence and between lack of education, violence, unemployment and poverty. So is affluence all that is needed to purge the violence in our midst? A glance at the so-called affluent societies suggests that this is a shaky premise. We can only conclude that we still know very little about the nature of human aggression, where it springs from, how it can be controlled and why control systems break down. At least this volume may contribute something towards an understanding of this problematic area of human behaviour.

## NOTES

1. *Football and the Fascists* (Contemporary Affairs Briefing, No.3); *Nazis in the Playground* (CAB, No.6); *Rock and the Right* (CAB No.8). Published by the Centre for Contemporary Studies, 1981.
2. Regina Yando and others, *Imitations, a developmental perspective*, John Willey and Sons, 1978.
3. Para. 16.13.
4. See 'Democratisation without Violence', Friedrich Hacker, Council of Europe, *Forum*, 4/85.

CHAPTER TWO

# SHORT MEMORIES

Street Violence in the Past and the Present

## Geoffrey Pearson

'Law-and-order' has loomed large in Britain's domestic politics
for a decade or more, and it is generally recognised as a key issue
in that decisive shift within the political culture which brought
Mrs. Thatcher's government to power in the late 1970s. The
concern with violence and disorder – hooliganism, street crime
and inner-city riots – acts as a vital metaphor of social change and
moral decline in Britain today. Invariably and unhesitatingly, the
problem is defined as something new and unprecedented – a
radical departure from the settled, stable traditions of the
'British way of life'. Then there follows the characteristic historical judgement that violence and disorder have rooted themselves
in the social landscape within the space of the past 20 or 30 years.
The notion of 'permissiveness' and moral laxitude is then in-
voked in order to explain why Britain's previously untroubled
history should have been so rudely and recently interrupted by
disorder on the streets and by violent crimes. Whereupon, fast on
the heels of this diagnosis of our social ills as the result of the
wastefully 'permissive' postwar years, there follows a regular
litany of complaint: the decline of family life and the break-up of
parental discipline; the weakening of authority in the public
spheres of the school and the criminal justice system; the corrupting influence of popular amusements such as television and
the 'video nasties'; and so on.

In the most recent round of this anguished debate, it has fallen
to the lot of Mr. Norman Tebbit, Chairman of the Conservative
Party, to trumpet these accusations against the ravages of 'permissiveness' and what he chose to call 'postwar funk' which had
dragged the nation down 'in the past thirty years'.[1] Even so, the

suddenness of this characteristically abbreviated timescale –
'twenty, thirty years ago' – should not disguise the fact that it
echoes a longer postwar history of familiar complaint. Already in
the late 1950s when the Conservative Party annual conference
debated the need for 'short, sharp shock' Detention Centres as a
remedy for Teddy Boy hooliganism, the problem was understood as the result of a 'lack of parental control in the home', the
'sex, savagery, blood and thunder' in films and television, the
'smooth, smug and sloppy sentimentalists' who had encouraged
'the leniency shown by the Courts' and a disrespect for the law,
and the other malevolently 'permissive' influences which were to
become the stock in trade of 'law-and-order' enthusiasts in the
hectic debates of the 1970s and 1980s. Indeed, at its annual
conference in 1958 it was already obvious that 'Over the past 25
years we in this country, through misguided sentiment, have cast
aside the word 'discipline', and now we are suffering from it'.[2]

It was only a few years later, in its mid-1960s publication *Crime
Knows No Boundaries*, that the Conservative Party would issue a
mature statement of its 'law-and-order' philosophy which connected the problems of crime and violence with the perceived
changes of the postwar world:

> We live in times of unprecedented change – change which
> often produces stress and social breakdown. Indeed the
> growth in the crime rate may be attributed in part to the
> breakdown of certain spontaneous agencies of social
> control which worked in the past. These controls operated
> through the family, the Church, through personal and local
> loyalties, and through a stable life in a stable society.[3]

It is of course the Conservative Party which has made most of
the running in Britain's postwar 'law-and-order' debates, and I
quote these examples of Conservative thinking from 20 and 30
years ago in order both to establish its lengthy postwar pedigree,
and to show up the hollowness of Mr. Tebbit's claim that public
life was any different 'thirty years ago'. Even so, I am not here to
score cheap political points – nor expensive ones for that matter.
Indeed, it is important to recognise that a very similar line of
argument flows from the Left, most notably in the writings
of Jeremy Seabrook, who has repeatedly and eloquently

denounced the way in which the 'get rich quick' instincts of the postwar consumer society have encouraged the egoistic, 'I'm alright Jack' mentality which in turn, in this version of events, had led to the downfall of standards and the upsurge of irresponsible violence. By contrast, Seabrook would have us think of the older traditions of working-class communities, based upon solidarities and loyalties which kept the hooligan wolf from the door: the loyalties of kinship, neighbourliness and the shared assumptions of 'making ends meet'. And once again the change is seen as a very new development. 'As recently as thirty years ago', Seabrook writes in his book *Working Class Childhood*, 'that older experience was still relatively intact in the working class streets throughout the country.' Whereas under the impact of 'the more mobile and open experience of recent years', Seabrook sees a high price exacted in 'the sense of disturbance in many children, the violence and absence of direction'.[4]

Seabrook's judgement is as absent-minded as Norman Tebbit's, in that thirty years ago his arguments had already been well rehearsed by Richard Hoggart's evocative analysis of the weakening of popular culture in *The Uses of Literacy*. There, Hoggart described how in the mid-1950s the old 'full rich life' of the back streets had been displaced by the faceless mass entertainment culture of 'admass' – a 'candy floss' world of valueless values, 'sex in shiny packets' and a 'ceaseless exploitation of hollow brightness'. 'This regular, increasing and almost unvaried diet of sensation without commitment', Hoggart argued, would 'render its consumers less capable of responding openly and responsibly to life' and 'induce an underlying sense of purposelessness'. Its effects moreover were most easily discerned among the young – the 'juke box boys', as Hoggart called them, an early strain of Teddy Boy, 'boys between fifteen and twenty, with drape-suits, picture ties and an American slouch'.[5]

Each argument, whether from Left or Right, has its own postwar history. Each sees the product of the postwar years as a disfigurement of our social life of nightmare proportions. There are different intentions behind these complaints, to be sure. Jeremy Seabrook understands the damage to have been worked by the egoistic imperatives of market forces, whereas Norman Tebbit understands 'permissiveness' as a product of the sloppy

social democratic consensus of the postwar years which can only
be remedied by allowing an even looser rein to those same
market forces. But it is nevertheless the consensus which holds
the attention. A consensus which holds that crime and violence
should be understood as the result of destructive social changes
which have swept through Britain in the space of 'thirty years' –
whereby the socialist Seabrook arrives at a surprising agreement
with the Tory Tebbit, with whom it can be safely assumed he
would agree on nothing else at all.

### SINCE THE WAR: WHICH WAR WAS THAT?

Now, having established the consensus, what I wish to do is to call
into question this way of thinking about crime, violence and
disorder in our streets. I will do this by interrogating the historical
claims which are draped around public discussions of these
matters – according to which we not only hear a great deal about
the specifically 'postwar' nature of our problems, thereby
implying that in the 1920s and 1930s Britain was somehow
immune to the difficulties which trouble us now, but also about
what are often loudly broadcast as the 'Victorian values' from
which we have fallen away. I will argue that the true historical
record is not easy to reconcile with the dominant way in which our
'law-and-order' fears are organised. By contrast, I will show that
the actual history suggests to us something quite different.
Namely that our present difficulties are not at all unprecedented,
that there is a long history to these kinds of trouble, and that we
have terribly short memories.

Take for example the following two statements, each familiar
in its own way, on the problems visited upon us by 'permissiveness' in the 'postwar' world:

> The passing of parental authority, defiance of pre-war
> conventions, the absence of restraint, the wildness of
> extremes, the confusion of unrelated liberties, the whole-
> sale drift away from churches, are but a few characteristics
> of after-war conditions.[6]

And, then, again:

That's the way we're going nowadays. Everything slick and streamlined, everything made out of something else. Celluloid, rubber, chromium-steel everywhere ... radios all playing the same tune, no vegetation left, everything cemented over.... There's something that's gone out of us in these twenty years since the war.[7]

We know the arguments off by heart. The phrases run so easily off the tongue. But there is an immediate point of difficulty here, because these complaints against 'postwar' irresponsibility both come from *before* the Second World War. The first is from the writings of a Christian youth worker, James Butterworth, writing in 1932 about the sweeping changes of the 'postwar' years. The second is from George Orwell's pre-war novel, *Coming Up for Air*, in which its central character, grumpy old George Bowling, looked back to the joys of his lost boyhood 'before the war' – that is, before the Great War of 1914–18.

Nor was it only youth workers and fictional characters in novels who succumbed to this unhappy vision in the inter-war years. 'Post-War people, as compared with Pre-War people, have lost confidence in things human and divine', wrote F.W. Hirst in 1934 in his summary of *The Consequences of the War to Great Britain* 'The post-war generation suffers from a sort of inward instability.... There seems nowadays to be no desire to provide for the future or look beyond tomorrow.'[8] Writing on *The Law-Breaker* in 1933, Roy and Theodora Calvert believed that 'this rejection of conventional standards' and 'the greater freedom from constraint which is characteristic of our age' meant that 'We are passing through a crisis in morals'.[9] T.S. Eliot's writings were drenched in the same anxieties about an age of moral confusion. 'We have arrived', he thought, 'at a stage of civilisation in which the family is irresponsible ... the moral restraints so weak ... the institution of the family is no longer respected.' This, as Eliot defined it, was 'a total decline of culture'.[10] Another active focus of discontent was the 'Scrutiny' group gathered around F.R. Leavis at Cambridge which repeatedly thundered against 'this vast and terrifying disintegration' of social life.[11] 'Change has been so catastrophic', Leavis wrote in 1930, that 'the generations find it hard to adjust themselves to each other, and parents are helpless to deal with their children.' 'It is a breach of continuity that threatens', Leavis warned, 'It is a commonplace that we are being Americanised.'[12]

Fears of 'Americanisation' often figured in these troubled English discourses on 'postwar' social change – then as now. In the 1930s this fear was most forcibly registered in the response to the Hollywood movies, and from their very beginnings the silent movies had been condemned for 'the distorted, unreal, Americanised way of life presented'.[13] So, as early as 1913 an article in The Times on 'Cinematography and the Child' had warned of the inherent violence of the new amusement, in a manner quite indistinguishable from the contemporary debate on the 'video-nasties':

> Before these children's greedy eyes with heartless indis-crimination horrors unimaginable are ... presented night after night.... Terrific massacres, horrible catastrophes, motor-car smashes, public hangings, lynchings.... All who care for the moral well-being and education of the child will set their faces like flint against this new form of excitement.[14]

The silent movies, and then later the 'talkies', also invited the more specific charge that they encouraged imitative crime among the young – a complaint which we usually think of as belonging only to the television age, but which had been scrutinised with great thoroughness in the monumental report of the National Council of Public Morals on The Cinema as early as 1917.[15] More generally, however, the Hollywood cinema was understood to have had a morally unbalancing effect on the younger generation. As described by A.E. Morgan in his King George's Jubilee Trust report on The Needs of Youth in 1939, here on the silver screen was

> A Never-never land of material values expressed in terms of gorgeous living, a plethora of high-powered cars and revolvers, and unlimited control of power ... of unbridled desire, of love crudely sentimental or fleshly, of vast possessions, or ruthless acquisition, of reckless violence.... It is an utterly selfish world.... It is a school of false values and its scholars cannot go unscathed.[16]

Accompanying these all-too-familiar fears of a newly de-
moralising form of popular entertainment, other familiar
accusations were thrown against the nation's youth in the 1930s
which was understood to be associated with a galloping 'crime
wave'. Morgan, once again, recited this catalogue of complaint:

> Relaxation of parental control, decay of religious influence,
> and the transplantation of masses of young persons to new
> housing estates where there is little scope for recreation and
> plenty for mischief ... a growing contempt by the young
> person for the procedure of juvenile courts.... The
> problem is a serious challenge, the difficulty of which is
> intensified by the extension of freedom which, for better or
> worse, has been given to youth in the last generation.[17]

There was indeed a sharp increase in recorded juvenile crime
in the 1930s, which in some quarters was blamed upon the 'namby
pamby methods' of 'our drawing-room courts' which had been
adopted as a result of the legislative reforms of the 1933 Children
and Young Persons Act – which was abused in the 1930s for its
weakening influence in much the same way that the 1969
Children and Young Persons Act has been held responsible for
juvenile crime in our own time.[18] It was, then, in a context such as
this that in 1937 a correspondent in *The Times* could sum up an
uncannily familiar set of complaints about mounting crime and
dwindling authority:

> There has been a tendency of late to paint a rather alarming
> picture of the depravity of the youth of the nation....
> Headlines scream the menace of 'boy gangsters'. Elderly
> magistrates deplore the abandonment of their panacea,
> the birch ... by gloomy forebodings in the Press of the
> inevitably disastrous results of the leniency and weakness of
> the present day.[19]

Other headlines catch the eye from the newspapers in the 1920s
and 1930s which conflict with our accustomed judgements on this
'peaceful' era – 'DARING RAIDS BY BAG-SNATCHERS.
Widow Badly Injured and Robbed'; 'SCANDAL OF THE
SHEFFIELD GANG FEUDS ...Lenient Magistrates';
'TERROR GANGS TO BE WIPED OUT. Flogging Advocated

for Slashers and Mutilators'; 'RIOTOUS SCENES IN
SALFORD. Police in Conflict with Demonstrators';
'FOOTBALL FRACAS. Police Baton Charge on Stone
throwers'; 'ROWDIES AT IT AGAIN IN BRADFORD
ELECTION FIGHT – Another Meeting Wrecked';
'GANGSTERS IN SUBURBIA. Widening of the Flying Squad
Net'; 'PC's HORSE BLINDED. Victim of Brush with the
Unemployed'; 'WOMAN INJURED BY VIOLENT BAG-
SNATCHER'; 'POLICE CALLED AT THREE FOOTBALL
MATCHES'; 'VANDALS AT WORK'.[20]

The trouble which lay behind these news headlines was a
persistent undercurrent in most if not all of the British cities in the
1920s and 1930s. At its extreme gang warfare was not uncommon –
involving such bodies of men as the Mooney Gang and the Park
Brigade from Sheffield which was nick-named 'Little Chicago';
the notorious Sabini gang in London; the 'Brummagem Boys'
from Birmingham – whose activities centred on racketeering and
protectionism, street-gambling schools and the control of racecourse meetings.[21] Meanwhile at the mundane level of everyday
life there was little respect for the law in many slum districts, and
policing in these quarters was so irregular and spasmodic that they
amounted to what we now call 'no go' areas. Violence could flare
around police attempts to suppress street-gambling schools or
when they intervened to douse the high spirits of Guy Fawkes
Night or rowdy gatherings of youths, and in one account of the
street life of the period the enforcement of the Street Betting Acts
is described as a particularly volatile flash-point whereby attempts
to arrest a bookie's runner 'always risked provoking a small riot'.[22]
The writings of youth club workers from this era – Butterworth's
*Clubland* (1932), Hatton's *London's Bad Boys* (1931) and
Secretan's *London Below Bridges* (1934) – are also teeming with
rowdy incident, outbreaks of hooliganism, shoplifting sprees,
youngsters terrorising old ladies, foul language, youth club riots
and vandalism.[23] And in the Mass Observation study, *The Pub
and the People*, which was based on fieldwork in Bolton in the late
1930s, we glimpse something of the rowdy bonhomie of the
working class weekend, together with 'the high point of mass
drunkenness' during the exodus from the northern industrial
towns to breezy Blackpool:

Along promenade the air is full of beersmell, that overcomes sea-smell. A swirling, moving mass of mostly drunken people, singing, playing mouth organs, groups dancing about. Chaps fall over and their friends pick them up cheerfully and unconcernedly. At one point a young man falls flat on his face, his friend picks him up and puts him over his shoulder, and lurches away with him. Immediately a fight starts among four young men: the crowd simply opens up to give them elbow room as it flows by; some stop to look on. One of the fighters is knocked out cold and the others carry him to the back of a stall and dump him there. Back streets are not so densely crowded, but even more drunks. In a litter of broken glass and bottles a woman sits by herself being noisily sick.[24]

Faced with an eye-witness account such as this, one immediately wants to ask, 'But where are the police?' And the same question would occur to us if we were to visit football stadiums in the inter-war period, where the police do not appear to have maintained the mass presence to which we have become accustomed. However, this did not mean that the crowds were quietly disciplined gatherings of serene working-class men in flat caps, as is usually supposed in the nostalgia which is heaped upon the history of professional football. Crowd disturbances and unruly behaviour – involving pitch-invasions and attacks on referees and players – had been a characteristic feature of the game since its beginnings as a spectator sport in the late nineteenth century, and disciplinary action was taken by the football authorities on numerous occasions because clubs failed to exercise proper control at their grounds. In 1921, for example, the boys' section at Bradford Park Avenue had been closed down for three months after the referee had been pelted with missiles, and in the early 1920s fierce North London rivalries between Arsenal and Tottenham Hotspur flared into open street battles in which some of the more fanatical supporters were armed with iron bars and knives. In the mid-1930s the Football Association found it necessary to issue a memorandum on 'rough play' because of the supposedly increasing use of foul tactics by players, and at the same time crowd behaviour also excited some interest in the press. In one typical incident in November 1936 Wolverhampton

Wanderers fans had attacked visiting Chelsea players, and there were also violent scenes after the game when an angry crowd of 2,000 people mobbed the officials' entrance in protest at the club's policy of selling its better players. The following week police had to be called to quell disturbances at a number of grounds – including Middlesborough and Upton Park where the referee was again attacked – and *Reynolds's News* thought it something of a joke that 'the FA will soon have to issue another "rough play" memorandum – this time to the spectators!'[25]

If none of this can be reconciled with nostalgic recollections of pre-war stability and order in Britain's streets, then what of the political scene and more formal aspects of public order? This is in fact a question which we should not find necessary to ask, if it were not for the profound historical amnesia which has settled around the actualities of pre-war social life: because why, when all is said and done, do we imagine that Parliament felt obliged to pass the Public Order Act in 1936? The immediate precipitating events to the Act, which gave the police powers to ban processions and prohibited the use of uniforms, had been street fights between fascists and anti-fascists which culminated in the 'Battle of Cable Street' when a march by Sir Oswald Mosley's British Union of Fascists through the Jewish quarters of the East End of London was confronted by a huge crowd estimated by the police at 100,000 people. Even so, there had already been many serious public order incidents in earlier years which were associated with the Hunger Marches and other protests of the employed which not infrequently resulted in violent clashes with the police.[26]

In one of the earliest incidents of this kind, in 1921, the Recorder of Liverpool had publicly rebuked the city's police because of their use of 'most unnecessary violence' in a baton charge against a meeting of the unemployed at the Walker Art Gallery. And although the Chief Constable of Liverpool survived this controversy – believing the use of force to have been 'fully justified', and reminding his critics of the looting and disorder which had accompanied the abortive police strike in Liverpool in 1919, which was also a year of race riots in the city – similar troubles dogged the unemployed movement for the next ten years or more.[27]

Since the riots of Brixton and Toxteth in the summer of 1981, we have become accustomed to a heated controversy as to whether these events should be understood as a consequence of inner-city deprivation and unemployment – with a common assumption running through many of these arguments that the absence of similar disturbances during the Slump of the inter-war years disproves any possible connection between unemployment and social disorder.

It is all the more remarkable, then, and a further indication of our profound forgetfulness, that the riots of 1981 occurred on the fiftieth anniversay of what was very probably the most widespread outbreak of social disorder in the inter-war years, when in October 1931 violent clashes flared between the police and the unemployed, visiting more than 30 towns and cities in the following month or so. These confrontations were prompted by cuts in unemployment benefit which had been recently enacted, and the police led baton charges in Cardiff, London, Salford, Manchester, Blackburn, Glasgow and elsewhere. In Manchester where high-pressure fire-hoses were used against a section of the crowd in Piccadilly, and in Salford where there had been a pitched battle outside the Town Hall, the violence continued intermittently for some days in protest against arrests which had been made, causing the police to place a guard on shops, banks, court-houses and public buildings. In Glasgow shops were smashed and looted after mounted police had scattered a crowd of 50,000 people in Glasgow Green, whereupon the police were bombarded with missiles hurled from tenement buildings and there was a fresh outbreak of looting in the Garngad district.[28]

In the following weeks and months confrontations between the police and the unemployed became a regular occurrence, as violence erupted in many different towns and cities. Early in 1932 there was renewed fighting with the police in Glasgow and in Keighley, as well as in parts of London when the unemployed defied a police ban on protest meetings outside Labour Exchanges, and in Rochdale where the army reserve was called out to defend the Town Hall. And so it went on through the winter months – as far afield as Coventry, Great Harwood, Shoreditch and Barnsbury in London, Wallsend, Kirkcaldy, Leeds and Stoke-on-Trent.

During the spring and summer months of 1932 there was a lull, whereupon in September and October there was a renewal of bitter fighting and rioting in Birkenhead, West Ham, Croydon, North Shields and Belfast, as well as in connection with the Hunger March of that year as it converged on London. In Belfast troops and armoured vehicles were used against barricades which had been thrown up, and two men were shot dead and numbers of others wounded as the fighting continued for several days. But it was perhaps the Birkenhead riots of a few days earlier which caused the most alarm, not only because of their ferocity but also because of the common English tendency to view violence and bloodshed in Northern Ireland as an entirely normal affair. The events on Merseyside – which prompted a Parliamentary request for an enquiry into the conduct of the police, which was refused by the Home Secretary who took the view that the disturbances were the work of agitators and conspirators – were complex and confused, embracing several days and nights of disorder, numerous protest marches, baton charges, looting incidents, street battles, ambushes against the police as they tried to enter the poorer districts, and allegations of brutality during house-raids. Among the shops that were broken into and looted was the local Co-operative store – symbol of respectable working-class mutual aid – and it was reported that as the police tried to enter the narrow streets and alleyways of the docks area, women bombarded them from upstairs windows with ashcans, household furniture and an iron bedstead. This was a no-holds-barred confrontation, and reinforcements were brought in from Birmingham, Liverpool and elsewhere as the police attempted to regain control of the town. As the disturbances spread across the river Mersey to Liverpool, so they died down in Birkenhead – but not before the Public Assistance Committee had made concessions to the rioters by raising the scales for unemployment relief, a climb-down by the authorities which was to be repeated a few days later in Northern Ireland after the rioting in Belfast.[29]

It is not only the evidence of criminal violence, hooliganism and social unrest in the 1920s and 1930s which conflicts with the ways in which we are usually encouraged to remember these years. Another thing which requires an altered judgement on our part is that the era's response to the problems of crime and violence was often surprisingly tolerant and sympathetic – particularly where young offenders were concerned. This was reflected in the decisions of the courts, where slightly more than half of juveniles charged with indictable offences received a probation sentence in the 1930s, as well as in wide areas of public debate.[30] As one indication of this 'permissive' mood, we can take the remarks of Sir Robert Baden-Powell, the founder of the Boy Scout movement, at a conference in 1933 on juvenile crime and juvenile unemployment. There had been a perceived increase of youthful crime in the early 1930s, and in some quarters it was held that the high level of juvenile unemployment was responsible – and, of course, we know both the problem and the controversy, including that rather extreme version of events which puts all crime down to 'wickedness' which was not at all in evidence in the pre-war years. Baden-Powell's view of the matter, however, was that if it were true that crime had increased because of unemployment, this was 'rather a promising sign':

> To him it was rather a promising sign, because he saw in those banditry cases, robbery with violence, and smash and grab, little 'adventures'. There was still some spirit of adventure among those juveniles, and if that spirit were seized and turned in the right direction they could make them useful men.[31]

It had long been a feature of Baden-Powell's Boy Scout philosophy that crime and hooliganism were a sign of 'pluck' and 'spirit' among working-class youth, far preferable to the idle ways of smoking, betting and loafing on street corners.[32] And he was, of course, something of a maverick in his views on discipline and education which frequently took a quite outrageously libertarian turn – although these too were not uncommon in his age.[33] Nowadays, to dare suggest that youthful crime and hooliganism were signs of a 'plucky' refusal to be ground down by unemployment would be to risk public infamy. There has been a narrowing of moral options and responses in the postwar years, and we are now much less tolerant of this kind of behaviour. Maybe that is a good thing, although perhaps it is unwise to judge one age by the standards of another. For if we were to use our intolerance to measure the standards of the past, then amidst all our other wrong-headed notions about the pre-war years, we might arrive at the ridiculous conclusion that Sir Robert Baden-Powell was the 'Bernie Grant' of the 1930s. And that would never do.

## VICTORIAN VALUES: FROM CHARTISM TO HOOLIGANS

It seems quite clear that there is something deeply wrong with the ways in which we are usually encouraged to think of the pre-war years as a peaceful and orderly contrast to the difficulties of contemporary Britain. Rather, we find an uncanny familiarity in the 1920s and 1930s, both in terms of the complaints against declining standards and the actualities of street violence and disorder. A familiarity that is reinforced, moreover, by the way in which people were already looking back in the pre-war years across another war to the lost standards of the fondly remembered late Victorian and Edwardian era.

If the inter-war years do not live up to their reputation, what then of those 'Victorian values' about which we have begun to hear so much again in recent years, as if Victorian England were some gold-standard of untarnished moral worth from which as a nation we have fallen away?

It will be as well to say at once that there is something faintly silly about this appeal to 'Victorian' virtue. Not only was Victorian society profoundly undemocratic, it was also characterised by widespread and unbearable poverty, prolific vice and prostitution, while Queen Victoria's long reign was punctuated by frequent social unrest and violence. No sooner had the young Queen come to the throne in 1837 than the country was plunged into fearful disorder through the Rebecca riots of rural Wales and the Chartist agitations of the late 1830s and early 1840s, a convulsion so massive that according to one recent and authoritative judgement the Chartist rising of 1842 signalled 'the year in which more energy was hurled against the authorities than in any other of the nineteenth century'.[34] The stable 'Victorian' traditions got off to a good start, then, and throughout the 1840s and early 1850s middle-class anxieties ran high about what was seen as an epidemic of juvenile depravity – understood as a symptom of the break-up of family life in the manufacturing districts – and the violent threat of the so-called 'dangerous classes'.[35] During the same period, the newly formed police were faced with deep suspicion and open hostility in plebeian communities.[36] The fear of violent crime returned to respectable London in the late 1850s and early 1860s when panic swept through the metropolis as a result of the 'garotting' robberies, which prompted Parliament to reinstate flogging on the statute book almost as soon as it had been removed by the penal reforms of 1861.[37] The Fenian outrages of the late 1860s then coincided with agitation around electoral reform, symbolised by the 'Hyde Park railings affair' when an angry political assembly of 100,000 people smashed their way into the park – which was just one of the violent manifestations of the East End 'Rough' who troubled Matthew Arnold so deeply in his mid-Victorian classic, *Culture and Anarchy*, which appeared in 1869.[38] The 1870s witnessed a resurgence of mob violence at elections, which carried on for some years.[39] The end of the decade also saw the London burglary scare which, amidst fierce criticism of the inefficiency and corruption of the police, caused sufficient alarm to lead to the arming of the London police with revolvers for the first time in their history in 1883 – although this was against the advice of senior police officers who judged their constables to be 'men of excitable temperament', according to an internal memorandum, who were 'not to be trusted to use revolvers with discretion'.[40] The 1880s were a decade of turbulence: the riots of the 'Skeleton Army' against Salvationists in many southern towns; the emergence of the savage street-fighting 'Scuttler' gangs in Manchester and Salford; the famous battle of 'Bloody Sunday' in London's Trafalgar Square during the Queen's Jubilee Year in 1887; and the hysterical fears of the previous year when after the Carlton Club had been attacked and Piccadilly looted by a political march turned riot, the West End was placed on the alert for several days against the possibility of an uprising of the unemployed.[41] Finally, the 'Gay Nineties' – a decade which saw the military open fire on strikers for the last time in our history, together with the Diamond Jubilee of 1897 which was also the year of the bitter engineers' lock-out when the employers went on the offensive against the 'new Unionism' – and which then came to an end on an appropriate note, with the arrival of a new word into the English vocabulary: 'Hooliganism'.[42]

The word 'Hooligan' made a sudden entrance into common English usage during the hot summer of 1898, after an excessively rowdy August Bank Holiday celebration in London which had resulted in dozens of people being brought before the courts on charges of drunkenness, disorderly conduct, assaults on police officers, street robberies and fighting. It was 'something like organised terrorism in the streets', thought *The Times*, which also wondered whether it was the result of the unusually hot weather which might 'fire the blood of the London rough or street arab, with an effect analogous to that of a southern climate upon the hot-blooded Italian or Provencal'. Naturally enough, the possibility was also considered that something so obviously 'un-English' might have to be curbed by un-English means:

> In Continental cities, or in the free Republic of America, they have very little scruple about calling out troops and shooting down organised disturbances of the peace . . . But if we do not adopt Continental methods of dealing with street lawlessness . . . if we do not wish our police to be formidable as an armed force, we must not grudge an increase in their numbers.[43]

One of the more worrying aspects of these Bank Holiday outrages is that they highlighted fierce traditions of resistance to the police in working-class neighbourhoods, whereby policemen attempting to make an arrest in the open street would be set upon by large crowds – sometimes numbering two or three hundred people – shouting 'Rescue! Rescue! and 'Boot 'im!'. Because the English fair-play habit of fighting with the fists and not with the feet would already seem to have entered eclipse in late Victorian England, as evidenced by frequent headlines such as ' "Boot 'em" at Waterloo', 'They Play Football with a Man', 'Kick a Man like a Football' and 'Kicked to Death'.[44]

The dangers of the London streets in the late 1890s and early 1900s can be judged against the fact that each year, according to the annual reports of the Metropolitan Police Commissioner, one in four of London's policemen were assaulted in the course of their duty, and one-tenth of these would be on the sick-list for a fortnight or more.[45] Nor was this because the police deliberately sought out trouble in the more notorious districts. On the contrary, the circumstances of policing in this period of history were such that the police often found it necessary to turn a blind eye to legal infringements. For example, in an internal memorandum on the difficulties of enforcing what were described as 'petty offences' under the Police Acts, in this case two men fighting in the street while surrounded by a crowd, a police superintendent offered the following opinion in 1900:

> It is often quite impossible for one constable to apprehend persons who are fighting and are surrounded by a rough crowd and to attempt to do so would in many cases lead to a much more serious breach of the peace.[46]

Offences such as this were not viewed with anything like the seriousness that we now attach to them, so that in 1899 the Metropolitan Police Commissioner could happily report that although there had been a sharp increase in recorded crime, 'it is satisfactory to note that the arrests were mostly for offences of a trivial nature, such as drunkenness, disorderly conduct, offences against the Police Acts, common assaults etc.' and he felt it necessary to distinguish these 'trivial' acts of hooliganism from the proper work of his criminal department.[47]

This is not at all the way in which we would expect a chief constable nowadays to respond to the problems of disorderly conduct, assaults and hooliganism. What must astonish us even more, however, are the kinds of things which could be classified as 'common assault' in this period of history and the punishments which were felt to be appropriate. One Sunday evening in the summer of 1898, for example, as a railway excursion returned from Herne Bay to London Bridge, a bottle-fight broke out among the holiday-makers and a man was killed in the fighting. The only action taken as a result of this fatality, however, was that three men were brought before the magistrate the following day on a non-indictable charge of 'assault', where they were fined 20 shillings each and required to pay the doctor's bill on the dead man.[48] In another case, widely reported in the press as 'The Alleged Hooligan Tragedy', a 32-year-old man by the name of Carey died from injuries which had been sustained, he said, when he was 'kicked to death by Hooligans in the Borough'. Witnesses to the event disagreed, however, saying that Mr. Carey had been involved in a fair 'stand-up' fight, but that when some others joined in he had taken a fall and struck his head on a tramline. Similarly, Mr. Burke was a 56-year-old man who died after claiming that he had been set upon by a gang in the street, but the verdict of the coroner's hearing was merely that he had died from accidental causes.[49]

Life was evidently cheap in the streets of late Victorian London, and it would appear that law enforcement was so irregular that some neighbourhoods were virtually un-policed. Publicans in these areas who complained too often about violence on their premises were said to have 'got the name among the police of being "fussy" ', and in one revealing incident a man who reported to the police that he had been assaulted and robbed by a gang complained bitterly that the police had refused to take him seriously and that when he persisted with his complaint he had been arrested on a charge of drunkenness and locked in a cell for the night.[50] Allegations of apathy by the police, although not always so colourfully described, were widespread at the time of the 'Hooligan' outcry and there were moves in some quarters towards vigilante action.[51] Some indication of the extent of the 'dark figure' of unreported hooliganism in these 'no-go' areas can be gained from a small-scale police experiment in 1903, in which a handful of men were stationed on special duties in a few police districts in order to combat street rowdyism. In little more than twelve months 3,499 arrests and summonses were made, mostly in seven police districts, with the heaviest concentration in 'L' district where four men made 1,067 arrests in the same period.[52]

From the late 1890s until the outbreak of the Great War an entirely familiar pattern of complaint was arranged around this question of violence on the streets, which embraced allegations against the decline of moral standards, the break-up of family life, the weakening of traditional discipline and the unparalleled unruliness of the younger generation. The Stipendiary Magistrate for Brighton summed up these 'tendencies of modern life' in 1898:

> The tendencies of modern life incline more and more to ignore or disparage social distinctions, which formerly did much to encourage respect for others and habits of obedience

and discipline . . . the manners of children are deteriorating . . . the child of today is coarser, more vulgar, less refined, than his parents were.[53]

In the following year 'the break-up or weakening of family life' was on the editorial agenda of *The Times*, no less than 'the break-up or impairment of the old ideas of discipline or order' in the cities.[54] That young people 'have tasted too much freedom' or 'had no idea of discipline or subordination' was a tireless accusation.[55] They lived 'a bandit life away from their homes', said a government report of 1910, 'free of all control'.[56] 'Speaking generally', according to Reginald Bray in 1911, 'the city-bred youth is growing in a state of unrestrained liberty.'[57] Helen Bosanquet agreed. It was, for her, 'a somewhat unlovely characteristic of the present day' to find in young people 'a prevailing and increasing want of respect towards their elders, more especially, perhaps, towards their parents'.[58] Not everyone was sure, however, that the parents deserved respect. The Physical Deterioration Committee of 1904 found 'no lack of evidence of increasing carelessness and deficient sense of responsibility among the younger women of the presnt day . . . This testified to by a crowd of witnesses' – as indeed it was.[59]

The elementary system of education provided by the Board Schools (also known jokingly as the 'Bored Schools') were in like manner criticised for their frail discipline. Many a boy, wrote E.J. Urwick in 1904, was 'a Jekyll in the classroom, a Hyde in the street'.[60] The modern system of elementary education was even blamed for having created the problem of rowdyism and hooliganism, as when Mr. James Kerr, Medical Officer of the London School Board, defined the newly-named Hooligan as 'a product of the Education Act', an opinion that was echoed elsewhere.[61]

The Music Halls also received their portion of blame as a breeding ground for imitative crime, or what we would now call 'copy-cat' behaviour. Asking 'how far a Music Hall programme may be held to encourage lawlessness', a Board School Manager writing on 'Hooliganism and the Halls' in *The Times* in the late 1890s felt sure that the great majority of Music Hall songs 'could never have been written if the loafer, the liar, the drunkard, the thief, and the sensualist had been regarded as subjects unfit to be glorified in song'.[62] 'This kind of garbage is part and parcel of the repertoire of nearly every Music Hall in the Kingdom', asserted another critic who thought that the 'spicy' jokes and suggestive songs so much in favour in the Halls 'put decency and clean-living at a discount, and glorify immorality all round'.[63] From Manchester early in the new century Charles Russell recounted how 'horrible murders and terrible tragedies were enacted before the footlights', leading to 'so many instances of violence on the part of young men in the backstreets of the city'.[64] Soon, it would be the turn of the early silent movies to be condemned in equal terms as 'a direct incentive to crime' and 'a grave danger to the community . . . responsible for the downfall of many young people'.[65]

Whether or not Music Hall entertainments did encourage 'copy-cat' street violence, some of the lower-class Halls were themselves the occasion for rowdyism and rough horse-play among the audience, from which we can learn a great deal about popular morality at this time in history. For example, we hear of the antics of the 'gallery boys' in the Victorian Music Halls and attempts to suppress them by the police and theatre managements, both because of the trouble which they caused by harassing audiences and local shopkeepers, and also their custom of levying a 'tax' on theatre-goers who occupied the better seats by making them pay a double entry fee.[66] When Robert Blatchford described a visit to one of the Halls in the late 1890s he left us a vivid portrait of the audience of dockers, costers, labourers and mechanics, together with their wives and sweethearts and babies in arms – the lads at the back keeping up a chorus of 'chirruping' to interrupt the events on the stage, some pelting those in the pits below with orange pips and other missiles, and everyone howling with laughter at the vulgar banter of the crowd. Blatchford did not reckon much to the artistic quality of the old-fashioned melodrama which was the main attraction, but 'very significant were the marks of popular interest and favour':

> When the police arrested the hero in the streets and a rescue was attempted by the denizens of the Boro', the audience became quite excited, many of them stood up, and all fell into the spirit of the scene – sympathy being manifestly against the law.[67]

Nor were such sympathies confined to the stage, as P.C. 158 Young found to his disadvantage when called to a disturbance at the Battersea Empire Music Hall one January evening in 1909, where his arrival was greeted with the battle-cry of 'Give it to the copper!' and he was assaulted by a gang of youths.[68] The record of assaults on police, violent resistance to arrest and rescue attempts by rough crowds provides a consistent thread from the 1890s to the outbreak of the Great War, whenever policemen were called to assist at Music Halls, public houses, racecourse meetings or other places of popular amusement.[69]

Football, too, was already on the boil and there is a well documented history of pitch invasions, attacks on referees and players, together with fighting between rival fans throughout the latter part of the nineteenth century and into the new century.[70] 'The dirty-nosed little rascals who spoil every football match they go to' went down in a referee's notebook in 1884 after he had been ill-treated by a Bolton crowd, and in the same year a Northern sporting rag described how 'a continuous hail of empty bottles' had showered the pitch during a recent game.[71] Writing on 'The Football Madness' a decade later, Ernest Ensor was particularly shocked by the epidemic of excitement among the fans: 'A constant attendant at great football matches must have seen more than once a large crowd *vertere pollicem* in a manner which made him thankful that murder is illegal'.[72] It was not only the violence of the crowds, but their 'warped sporting instincts' which impressed Ensor, who strung together yet another familiar catalogue of complaint against the commercialisation of sport, the adoption of foreign coaching methods, excessive profession-alism and the constant use of foul tactics in order to win at all costs, and a wholesale corruption of sporting values.[73] And here too at the football stadiums was Robert Baden-Powell, brooding over the temperamental downfall of the English race in the first edition of *Scouting for Boys* where he likened the crowd behaviour to that of the 'unmanly' young Romans who contri-buted to the downfall of Rome by loafing around the circus entertainments and 'paid men to play their games for them so that they could look on without the fag of playing, just as we are doing in football now':

Thousands of boys and young men, pale, narrow-chested,
hunched up, miserable specimens, smoking endless cigar-
ettes, numbers of them betting, all of them learning to be
hysterical as they groan or cheer in panic unison with their
neighbours – the worst sound of all being the hysterical
scream of laughter that greets any little trip or fall of a
player. One wonders whether this can be the same nation
which had gained for itself the reputation of being a stolid,
pipe-sucking manhood, unmoved by panic or excitement,
and reliable in the tightest of places.[74]


This supposed temperamental shift in the English character
was widely noted in the writings of the late 1890s and early 1900s.
It showed itself in 'a certain temper of fickle excitability' according
to Charles Masterman as he attempted to define the problem of
the 'new race' of the 'City-type' and 'the "street-bred" people of
the twentieth century'.[75] Warning of 'a canker at the heart of the
people that will surely destroy it', another commentator writing
under the cloak of anonymity in 1912 believed that 'the first stage
of decay has already been reached when the stolid, God-fearing
puritan of two-and-a-half centuries ago has given place to the
shallow, hysterical cockney of today'.[76] There was 'a wild spirit
of unrest abroad', as Reginald Bray understood matters, which
was quite different from the 'deliberate slowness in action' which
was 'once the characteristic of the Englishman'. 'The crowd of
the town in a moment flashes into a delirious mob', he continued,
believing that 'the invention of the new term "Mafficking" is
alone sufficient to indicate the extent of the transformation.'[77]
And there had indeed been editorial musings in *The Times* that
'to "Maffick" is not really congenial to the British character',
with the further possibility that 'our national character was
changing for the worse'.[78]

   Even so, perhaps the most eloquent testimony to the feeling of
the age was the adoption of those un-English, Irish-sounding
words – 'Hooligan' and 'Hooliganism' – in order to describe the
turbulent street gangs of late Victorian London. The precise
origins of the words remain obscure, although we can be certain
that they emerged from out of London's popular culture of the

1890s where they were probably first publicised in a Music Hall
song by the comedians O'Connor and Brady:

> Oh, the Hooligans! Oh, the Hooligans!
> Always on the riot, cannot keep them quiet.
> Oh, the Hooligans! Oh, the Hooligans!
> They are the boys
> To make a noise
> In our backyard.[79]

After these humble beginnings, very little is heard of the word
until it was thrust into the headlines in the wake of the Bank
Holiday excitements of the late summer of 1898 when throughout
August and September the newspapers were suddenly awash
with stories of gang fights and stabbings, assaults, street robberies
and other 'Hooligan' outrages. A typical pattern of disorder
quickly came to be associated with the newly-named 'Hooligans'.
They were regularly described as engaged in pitched battles
among themselves – Chelsea Boys against Fulham Boys in a
punch-up at Cheyne Walk, for example, or Margaret Street
against Chapel Street – as well as wrecking coffee stalls and pubs,
cluttering up the pavements in noisy gatherings, or assaulting and
sometimes robbing innocent by-standers. 'Some dozen boys, all
armed with sticks and belts, wearing velvet caps, and known as
the "Velvet Cap Gang", walking along', is how *The Daily
Graphic* described one such gang from Battersea, 'pushing people
off the pavement, knocking at shop doors and using filthy
language.' And then, a few days later from another part of
London: 'A gang of roughs, who were parading the roadway,
shouting obscene language, playing mouth organs, and pushing
respectable people down. The young ruffians were all armed
with thick leather belts, on which there were heavy brass buckles.'
Or, a couple of years later under the headline 'HOOLIGANS
AT HACKNEY', there is a report of a crowd of 30 people
'shouting disgusting language and knocking on the shutters of
shops with sticks . . . Quite a riot ensued, and sticks, stones, and
beer cans were thrown in all directions'.[80]

The words 'Hooligan' and 'Hooliganism' quickly became the
controlling terms in the debate on street crime and disorderly

conduct, even though at first it was not at all clear what the new words meant. But when the dust had settled and respectable England summoned up the courage to look the danger in the face, it transpired that the original Hooligans were what we would now call a 'youth culture'. Bell-bottom trousers cut tight at the knee and with a tasteful buttoned vent in the leg; colourful neck scarves and a distinctive style of cap; boots said in some quarters to be toe-plated with iron and calculated to 'kill easily'; ornamental leather belts with designs worked in metal pins; and a characteristic 'donkey fringe' hair cut: these were the elements of the London Hooligan style.[81]

In other cities, youths with the same clothes (and the same street-fighting habits) were known and feared by different names. In Manchester there were the 'Scuttlers', where the name and the style went back at least until the late 1880s, who were followed by a new generation calling themselves 'Ikes' or 'Ikey Lads'. In Birmingham the gangs were known as 'Peaky Blinders' or as 'Sloggers', and similar dress styles and violent gang loyalties were known in far-away Australia as 'Larrikins' and 'Larrikinism'.[82]

In London some of the local gangs had improvised stylistic details which asserted their local identity: the 'Velvet Cap Gang' from Battersea, or the 'Plaid Cap Brigade' from Poplar. There were also trendsetters among the Hooligans, and one young man appeared before a London police court in 1898 with what sounds remarkably like the Mohican hair-cut which was briefly popular among some of the more outlandish Teddy Boys in the 1950s and re-surfaced with the Punk styles of the late 1970s and 1980s: 'His hair had been clipped as closely as possible to the scalp, with the exception of a small patch on the crown of the head, which was pulled down over the forehead to form a fringe'.[83] 'The appearance of the witness caused some amusement in court', we were told, and there can be little doubt that if this way-out young man were to turn up on the streets of one of our cities today with his shaven head and tufted crown, then he would be heralded as a woeful sign of an unparalleled degeneration among the nation's youth.

Not everyone was agreed, however, that the Hooligans were quite such a threat as was generally assumed. It was 'press-manufactured Hooliganism', according to the distinguished

London Police Court Missioner Thomas Holmes, and elsewhere the affair was dismissed as 'silly season sensationalism' by sections of the press such as Northcliffe's new *Daily Mail*.[84] Because if the London police were widely accused of playing the matter down, it is equally true that the popular press was enjoying a Hooligan heyday. Charles Booth's massive survey of London life also urged caution: 'Hooliganism has been exaggerated by the press . . . so say our witnesses'.[85]

Without question the greatest exaggerations came around the commonly expressed fear that Hooligan gangs were regularly in possession of pistols and revolvers which they used in their street fights. The regulations for the sale of firearms were quite haphazard during these years, and there is every reason to believe that guns did sometimes fall into the hands of young men and boys in the slum quarters. The available evidence suggests, however, that the view put forward in the popular press that the armed Hooligan was a constant menace in the city streets was somewhat unbalanced.[86] Even so, whatever the substance to these delirious rumours, they indicate clearly enough the enormity of the fear of the unsafe streets in late Victorian London.

If the idea of regular armed combat in the streets with firearms describes the magnified fears of street violence, rather than the actualities, then it must be said at once that the actualities were themselves quite bad enough. Victorian cities pulsed with a rowdy and violent street culture. There was the tradition of 'holding the street', for example, a violent territorial ritual glimpsed by Walter Besant in 1901, whereby youths in working class neighbourhoods blocked their home street to all strangers:

> The boys gather together and hold the street; if anyone ventures to pass through it they rush upon him, knock him down, and kick him savagely about the head; they rob him as well . . . The boys regard holding the street with pride.[87]

Or there was the 'Scuttle', as described from Newton Heath in Manchester in 1890: a 'pitched battle' of between 500 and 600 youths, waged with the buckle-ends of belts, stones and powerful catapults, knives and iron bars.[88] Or, finally, from that fateful August Bank Holiday in 1898 which bequeathed to us the word

'Hooligan' itself, we stumble across what is described as a 'free fight' in the Old Kent Road which consumed the energies of some 200 people in the mutual embrace of a kicking contest.[89] The streets of Victorian cities were, from time to time, a veritable rough-house and to pretend otherwise is a sad delusion.


PRESENT TENSE, PAST PERFECT AND THE
SOCIAL QUESTION

The original 'Hooligan' gangs of the late Victorian cities were not the first time that street violence had manifested itself in Britain, although this was not entirely obvious to everyone at the time. Indeed, the dominant view was that the coining of the new term 'Hooliganism' had been made necessary precisely because of the emergence of a new phenomenon on the streets. We need only think of the adoption of the new word 'mugging', in Britain in the 1970s, to characterise a 'new' problem – whereas of course street robbery is a very old problem – in order to understand something of the social processes at work. It is, then as now, that familiar historical amnesia which obliterates all signs of incohesion in the past in order to dwell all the more fearfully upon the troubles of the present.

Nevertheless, this history of social violence and its associated discontents can be traced back not only to the beginning of the Victorian era, but also beyond the great urban and industrial transformations of the nineteenth century to what is often imagined to have been the sleepy tranquillity of 'Merrie England'. The pre-industrial social landscape was vastly different, of course, but supplied in merriment by the gin-shop and held in check by the gallows, 'Merrie England' offers no more by way of comfort to backward-looking nostalgia than anything that we have encountered so far. In the countryside there was the persistent interruption of the 'crowd' – in the shape of food riots most commonly, but also through the burning of hay-ricks and barns, agitation around the enclosure of the land, machine-breaking and other forms of violence and disorder.[90] In the towns, too, and particularly in London there was the threat of the 'Mob' – a word which itself originated in the 1680s – as well as the unruly traditions of apprentices, the lawless antics of street gangs with such colourful names as the Mohocks, Hawcubites, Scowrers, Nickers and Dead Boyes, together with the common ruffians who so much troubled Henry Fielding in his *Enquiry into the Causes of the Late Increase of Robbers* in 1751 which he understood as the result of 'luxury among the vulgar' which had led to 'an Impatience of Discipline and Corruption of morals' among the lower orders.[91]

What does this long and often repetitious history signify? It is certainly not easy to reconcile with the prevailing view that there has been a recent and unprecedented downfall of standards which has resulted in an equally unprecedented upsurge of violence on the streets. If only because there is nothing whatsoever unprecedented about the complaints which have been brought repeatedly against the alleged deteriorations of the present, compared uninvitingly against the lovingly remembered (but hopelessly falsified) perfections of the past. Nor in the view that our streets have been recently plunged into a state of previously unparalleled disorder. What we find by contrast is a long, connected history of fearful complaint and controversy on these matters. A history, moreover, in which each successive generation has understood itself to be standing on the brink of a radical discontinuity with the remembered past.

It is abundantly clear, then, that there is no 'Golden Age' of civility from which we have recently departed because of the so-called 'permissiveness' of the postwar years. When they are put to the test of historical ratification, our contemporary fears of declining standards quite simply fail. If anything, in the course of the twentieth century our streets have become more orderly – and not less orderly – and we forget that to our cost.

How can we then account for the fact, however, that one of the indisputable realities in Britain today is a widespread fear of violent crime? Indeed, the notion of the 'fear of crime' is increasingly discussed in policy contexts as a problem in its own right, quite separate from the actual incidence of crime.[92] Is this 'fear of crime' simply a delusion or some kind of media-induced 'moral panic'? And if not, then what is the relationship between the fear of crime and the history which I have described?

What this history says to us is by no means unambiguous. It is necessary, for example, to disentangle the different levels at which the 'fear of crime' works, and to distinguish the different actors in the history, speaking with different voices, and with different purposes in mind. On the one hand there are the fears of ordinary people who are most likely to be the actual victims of crime, especially if they live in socially deprived urban areas.[93] These people's fears are quite different from the litany of complaint which has issued from moral and political elites down the ages, and where the preoccupation with violence is often only a thinly disguised fearful contempt of the lower orders (the 'dangerous classes') themselves. And this is quite different again from the sensational news stories and headlines which so often distort and exaggerate the actualities of crime and violence. Although it must be said at once that there is that strange calculus in human affairs whereby people who might be quite afraid of crime and violence nevertheless enjoy reading about some of its more gruesome consequences in their daily newspaper.

If these different spheres of interest are disentangled, then we can begin to get some idea of the complexity of the notion of the 'fear of crime', requiring from us an equally varied response to the different levels of concern. So that the conclusion that the thesis of a 'permissive' deluge is historically flawed does not entail that the 'fear of crime' is necessarily false: it is not the actual existence of street violence that is at issue, but the historical apparatus that is arranged around it. Admittedly, as we have begun to learn more about patterns of criminal victimisation there are points of detail where the 'fear of crime' does not correspond to the actual risks, and where the fears appear excessive. A thoroughly bewildering aspect of the 'fear of crime' phenomenon, for example, as recently described in a Home Office study, is that it is 'an almost universal finding of research on fear, that those who least often become victims of crime are most often fearful'.[94] This is an area of controversy, however, and while the Home Office sponsored British Crime Surveys of 1982 and 1984 suggest that people generally exaggerate the risks of victimisation, the more localised crime surveys recently conducted in Merseyside and Islington in inner-London maintain that fears of victimisation are more closely related to the actual risks.[95] What is particularly interesting from these local surveys is how the public rank the seriousness of different kinds of crime, and where they think the priorities for policing should be. So that while burglary, sexual assault and street robbery were seen as high priority crimes, there was general agreement that street rowdyism by youths – which is such a powerful focus for discontents among 'anti-permissive' and 'law-and-order' lobbies – was very low down on the list.[96] This is as clear an indication as one might have of the need to disentangle the moral agenda as defined from on high, from the fear of crime as expressed on the street.

There is nothing in this history, then, which should be taken to minimise the seriousness of the difficulties which we experience in the present day. Rather, it is a question of re-thinking what these difficulties amount to. The long, entrenched history of street violence and disorder shows perhaps how much more difficult it will be to dislodge or ameliorate the problem, than if it were true that it had sprung from nowhere 'in the past thirty years' or 'since the war'. It is commonplace slogans such as these which in fact trivialise the problem, in that they fail to grapple with – or even to acknowledge – the weight of tradition and history which bears down upon our present troubles. Long-standing social difficulties and disputes are not resolved by short, sharp remedies such as those in favour with the 'anti-permissive' lobby and 'law-and-order' enthusiasts. They require instead the long haul of social reform and reconstruction. They require from us a confidence in the future and in the rising generation, rather than that dismal cultural pessimism which can see only the faults of the young, and which is cast over them like a shroud in Britain today. The task also requires what the Church has recently and aptly re-defined for us as a continuing 'faith in the city', and a corresponding rejection of the anti-urban sentiments which have for so long plagued English middle-class values.[97] Indeed, this tradition of anti-urbanism must under-write in some large measure the morally scandalous neglect of the mass unemployment by which so many of our major industrial towns and cities have been laid to waste. And this in fact is the final requirement if we are to understand and begin to combat the violence in our society: a recognition that social violence in modern Britain has its roots in the material circumstances of social deprivation, and that it does not come out of the leafy suburbs but out of the slums – just as it always did.

NOTES AND REFERENCES

1. *The Guardian*, 14 Nov. 1985.
2. *78th Annual Conference* (Conservative Political Centre, 1958), pp. 95–102.
3. *Crime Knows No Boundaries* (Conservative Political Centre, 1966), p. 11.
4. J. Seabrook, *Working Class Childhood* (Gollancz, 1982), p. 202.
5. R. Hoggart, *The Uses of Literacy* (Penguin, 1958), pp. 232, 246, 248.
6. J. Butterworth, *Clubland* (Epworth, 1932), p. 22.
7. G. Orwell, *Coming Up for Air* (Penguin, 1962 edn), pp. 27, 168.
8. F.W. Hirst, *The Consequences of the War to Great Britain* (Oxford University Press, 1934), p. 74.
9. R. Calvert and T. Calvert, *The Law Breaker* (Routledge, 1933), pp. 60–1.
10. T.S. Eliot, *Notes Towards the Definition of Culture* (Faber & Faber, 1962 edn), pp. 26, 103–4.
11. F.R. Leavis and D. Thompson, *Culture and Environment* (Chatto & Windus, 1933), p. 87.
12. F.R. Leavis, *Mass Civilisation and Minority Culture* (Minority Press, 1930), pp. 6–7.
13. C.E.B. Russell, *The Problem of Juvenile Crime* (Oxford University Press, 1917), p. 6.
14. *The Times*, 12 April 1913.
15. National Council of Public Morals, *The Cinema* (Williams & Norgate, 1917). For a more detailed discussion, see G. Pearson, 'Falling Standards: A Short, Sharp History of Moral Decline' in M. Barker ed., *The Video Nasties: Freedom and Censorship in the Media* (Pluto, 1984).
16. A.E. Morgan, *The Needs of Youth* (Oxford University Press, 1939), p. 242.
17. Ibid., pp. 166, 191.
18. Cf. G. Pearson, *Hooligan: A History of Respectable Fears* (Macmillan, 1983), pp. 46–8, 216–17.
19. *The Times*, 4 Jan. 1937.
20. *Reynolds's News*, 11 Oct. 1931, 18 Oct. 1931, 1 Nov. 1931, 22 Sept. 1935, 29 Sept. 1935, 17 Nov. 1935, 15 Nov. 1936, 20 Dec. 1936; *Bradford Telegraph and Argus*, 22 Oct. 1931; *The Times*, 2 Oct. 1931; *Sheffield Mail*, 26 June 1923.
21. J.P. Bean, *The Sheffield Gang Wars* (Routledge & Kegan Paul, 1981).
22. J. White, 'Police and People in London in the 1930s', *Oral History*, vol.11, no.1, 1983, p. 38; J. White, 'Campbell Bunk: A Lumpen Community in London between the Wars', *History Workshop*, issue 8, 1979; J. White, 'The Summer Riots of 1919', *New Society*, 13 Aug. 1981.
23. S.F. Hatton, *London's Bad Boys* (Chapman & Hall, 1931); H.A. Secretan, *London Below Bridges* (Bles, 1931); Butterworth, *Clubland*, op. cit., pp.

39 ff.

24. Mass Observation, *The Pub and the People* (Gollancz, 1943), p. 248.

25. Pearson, *Hooligan*, op. cit., pp. 29–31; *Reynolds's News*, 15 Nov. 1936.

26. J. Stevenson and C. Cook, *The Slump* (Quartet, 1979), chs. 9–12.

27. Public Record Office, Home Office Papers, HO 45/11032/423878; *Daily Herald*, 3 Oct. 1921; R. May and R. Cohen, 'The Interaction between Race and Colonialism: A Case Study of the Liverpool Race Riots of 1919', *Race and Class*, vol.16, no.2, 1974.

28. *Yorkshire Post*, 2 Oct. 1931 and 3 Oct. 1931; *The Times*, 2 Oct. 1931, 17 Oct. 1931 and 19 Oct. 1931; Stevenson & Cook, *The Slump*, op. cit., p. 168; W. Hannington, *Unemployed Struggles 1919–1936: My Life and Struggles Amongst the Unemployed* (EP Publishing, 1973 edn), pp. 226–9.

29. Hannington, *Unemployed Struggles*, op. cit., pp. 233–41; Stevenson and Cook, *The Slump*, op. cit., pp. 169–73.

30. Pearson, *Hooligan* op. cit., pp. 40–8. Rather obviously, this tolerance was not shown in police reactions to unemployed workers' demonstrations during the inter-war years, which may have been because the actions of the unemployed lacked public legitimacy. For such an argument, see R. Geary, *Policing Industrial Disputes: 1893 to 1985* (Cambridge University Press, 1985).

31. *The Times*, 25 May 1933.

32. E.g. R. Baden-Powell, 'The Boy Scouts', *National Defence*, vol.4, Aug. 1910, p. 446; R. Baden-Powell, *Aids to Scoutmastership* (Jenkins, 1919), p. 31.

33. Pearson, *Hooligan*, op. cit., pp. 43–6, 110 ff.

34. D. Thompson, *The Chartists* (Temple Smith, 1984), p. 295; D. Williams, *The Rebecca Riots* (Wales University Press, 1955).

35. E.g. H. Worsley, *Juvenile Depravity* (Gilpin, 1849); T. Beggs, *An Enquiry into the Extent and Causes of Juvenile Depravity* (Gilpin, 1849); M. Hill, *Juvenile Delinquency* (Smith, Elder & Co, 1853); Pearson, *Hooligan*, op. cit., ch.7; G. Pearson, *The Deviant Imagination* (Macmillan, 1975), pp. 148 ff.

36. R.D. Storch, 'The Plague of Blue Locusts: Police Reform and Popular Resistance in Northern England, 1840–57', *International Review of Social History*, vol.20, no.1, 1975.

37. Pearson, *Hooligan*, op. cit., ch.6; J. Davis, 'The London Garotting Panic of 1862', in V.A.C. Gatrell *et al* eds., *Crime and the Law* (Europa, 1980); P.W.J. Bartrip, 'Public Opinion and Law Enforcement: The Ticket-of-Leave Scares in Mid-Victorian Britain', in V. Bailey ed., *Policing and Punishment in Nineteenth Century Britain* (Croom Helm, 1981).

38. M. Arnold, *Culture and Anarchy* (Cambridge University Press, 1960); Pearson, *Hooligan*, op. cit., pp. 124–8.

39. D.C. Richter, 'The Role of Mob Riot in Victorian Elections', *Victorian Studies*, vol.15, no.1, 1971.

40. Public Record Office, Metropolitan Police Commissioner, MEPO 2/163; Home Office, HO 45 9755/A60557; 'The Police Force Going to Pieces', *Vanity Fair*, 18 Jan. 1879; *Pall Mall Gazette*, 5 Aug. 1878.

41. For the 'Skeleton Army': Public Record Office, Home Office, HO 45 9629/A22415; HO 45 9625/A19890; HO 45 9636/A30742; HO 45 9638/ A32518; V. Bailey, 'Salvation Army Riots: The "Skeleton Army" and Legal Authority in the Provincial Town', in A.P. Donajgrodzki, ed., *Social Control in Nineteenth Century Britain* (Croom Helm, 1977); D.C. Richter, *Riotous Victorians* (Ohio University Press, 1981), ch.6. For 'Scuttlers': Pearson, *Hooligan*, op. cit., pp. 94–6; C.E.B. Russell, *Manchester Boys* (Manchester University Press, 1905); Public Record Office, Home Office, HO 45 9723/A51956. For 'Bloody Sunday' and the Carlton Club: G. Stedman Jones, *Outcast London* (Oxford University Press, 1971), pp. 291–6; Richter, *Riotous Victorians*, op. cit., chs. 8 and 9.

42. For the shooting of striking miners at Featherstone: Geary, *Policing Industrial Disputes*, op. cit., ch.2. For the origins of 'Hooligan' and 'Hooliganism': Pearson, *Hooligan*, op. cit., ch.5.

43. *The Times*, 17 Aug. 1898.

44. *South London Chronicle*, 27 Aug. 1898, 3 Sept. 1898, 15 Oct. 1898; *News of the World*, 2 Oct. 1898; *The Daily Graphic*, 3 Aug. 1898.

45. *Report of the Commissioner of the Police of the Metropolis 1898*, C. 9449 (HMSO, 1899), p. 28; *Report of the Commissioner of the Police of the Metropolis 1899*, Cd. 399 (HMSO, 1900), p. 31; *Royal Commission on the Duties of the Metropolitan Police*, vol.II, Minutes of Evidence, Cd. 4260 (HMSO, 1908), qu.79; Public Record Office, Metropolitan Police Commissioner, MEPO 2/531.

46. Public Record Office, Metropolitan Police Commissioner, MEPO 2/466.

47. *Report of the Commissioner . . . 1898*, op. cit., p. 8.

48. *South London Chronicle*, 27 Aug. 1898.

49. *South London Chronicle*, 1 Oct. 1898, 8 Oct. 1898 and 3 Sept. 1898; *News of the World*, 2 Oct. 1898.

50. *The Sun*, 3 Aug. 1898; *News of the World*, 14 Aug. 1898.

51. *The Sun*, 2 Aug. 1898 and 6 Aug. 1898; *South London Chronicle*, 6 Aug. 1898 and 13 Aug. 1898; *The Echo*, 11 Aug. 1898; *The Daily Graphic*, 22 Aug. 1898.

52. Public Record Office, Metropolitan Police Commissioner, MEPO 2/727.

53. *Juvenile Offenders* (Howard Association, 1898), pp. 22–3.

54. *The Times*, 6 Feb. 1899 and 16 Aug. 1899.

55. W.J. Braithwaite, 'Boys' Clubs', in E.J. Urwick, ed., *Studies Inter-Departmental Committee on Physical Deterioration*, vol.II, Minutes of Evidence, Cd. 2210 (HMSO, 1904), qu.2107.

56. *Report of the Departmental Committee on the Employment of Children Act 1903*, Cd. 5229 (HMSO, 1910), p. xxviii.

57. R.A. Bray, *Boy Labour and Apprenticeship* (Constable, 1911), p. 102.

58. H. Bosanquet, *The Family* (Macmillan, 1906), p. 310.

59. *Committee on Physical Deterioration*, op. cit., vol.I, Cd. 2175, p. 55.

60. Urwick, *Studies of Boy Life*, op. cit., p. 295.

61. *Report of the Royal Commission on Physical Training (Scotland)*, vol.II, Minutes of Evidence, Cd. 1508 (HMSO, 1903), qu.6059; *The Catholic Pulpit*, Sept. 1898; *The Daily Mail*, 11 Aug. 1898.

62. *The Times*, 26 Sept. 1898. Compare the lively riposte in the music hall trade magazine, *Music Hall and Theatre Review*, 7 Oct. 1898.
63. A. Wilson, 'Music Halls', *Contemporary Review*, vol.78, July 1900, p. 138.
64. Russell, *Manchester Boys*, op. cit., p. 94.
65. *The Times*, 25 Oct. 1913.
66. D.A. Reid, 'Popular Theatre in Victorian Birmingham', in D. Brady *et al*, eds., *Performance and Politics in Popular Drama* (Cambridge University Press, 1980); P. Bailey, 'Custom, Capital and Culture in the Victorian Music Hall', in R.D. Storch, ed., *Popular Culture and Custom in Nineteenth Century England* (Croom Helm, 1982).
67. R. Blatchford, *Dismal England* (Walter Scott, 1899), p. 37.
68. Public Record Office, Metropolitan Police Commissioner, MEPO 2/1238.
69. Public Record Office, Metropolitan Police Commissioner, MEPO 2/531; Pearson, *Hooligan*, op. cit., pp. 85–8.
70. W. Vamplew, 'Ungentlemanly Conduct: in T.C. Smout, ed., *The Search for Wealth and Stability* (Macmillan, 1979).
71. T. Mason, *Association Football and English Society 1863–1915* (Harvester, 1980), p. 162; *Football Field and Sports Telegram*, 27 Sept. 1884.
72. E. Ensor, 'The Football Madness', *Contemporary Review*, vol.74, Nov. 1898, p. 752.
73. Ibid., p. 754 and *passim*. See also C. Edwardes, 'The New Football Mania', *Nineteenth Century*, vol.32, 1892; Anon, 'Some Tendencies of Modern Sport', *Quarterly Review*, vol.199, 1904; Anon, 'Sport and Decadence', *Quarterly Review*, vol.212, 1909.
74. R. Baden-Powell, *Scouting for Boys* (Horace Cox, 1908), p. 338.
75. C.F.G. Masterman, ed., *The Heart of the Empire* (Fisher Unwin, 1902), pp. 7–8.
76. Anon, 'Religious Influences on the Adolescent', in J.H. Whitehouse, ed., *Problems of Boy Life* (King, 1912), p. 257.
77. R.A. Bray, *The Town Child* (Fisher Unwin, 1907), pp. 145–6.
78. *The Times*, 30 Oct. 1900.
79. *Music Hall and Theatre Review*, 26 Aug. 1898; *Notes and Queries*, Ninth Series, No.2, 17 Sept. 1898, p. 227.
80. *The Daily Graphic*, 15 Aug. 1898 and 25 Aug. 1898; *Morning Advertiser*, 16 Oct. 1900.
81. Pearson, *Hooligan*, op. cit., pp. 92–101.
82. Ibid., pp. 94 ff.
83. *The Daily Graphic*, 6 Aug. 1898.
84. 'The Police Court and its Problems: An Interview with Mr. Thomas Holmes', *The Young Man*, vol.15, 1901, p. 327; *South London Chronicle*, 6 Aug. 1898; *Manchester Evening News*, 18 Aug. 1898; *The Echo*, 11 Aug. 1898; *The Sun*, 3 Aug. 1898; *Music Hall and Theatre Review*, 7 Oct. 1898.
85. C. Booth, *Life and Labour of the People in London: Notes on Social Influences* (Macmillan, 1903), p. 139.
86. Pearson, *Hooligan*, op. cit., pp. 101–6.
87. W. Besant, *East London* (Chatto & Windus, 1901), p. 177.

88. Public Record Office, Home Office, HO 45/9723/A51956; A. Devine, *Scuttlers and Scuttling* (Guardian Print Works, 1890).
89. *The Times*, 16 Aug. 1898.
90. E.P. Thompson, 'The Moral Economy of the English Crowd in the Eighteenth Century', *Past and Present*, no.50, 1971; E.P. Thompson, *Whigs and Hunters* (Allen Lane, 1975); D. Hay *et al.*, *Albion's Fatal Tree: Crime and Society in Eighteenth Century England* (Allen Lane, 1975); J. Brewer and J. Styles, eds., *An Ungovernable People: The English and their Law in the Seventeenth and Eighteenth Centuries* (Hutchinson, 1980); A. Charlesworth, ed., *An Atlas of Rural Protest in Britain 1548–1900* (Croom Helm, 1983); G. Pearson, 'Goths and Vandals: Crime in History', *Contemporary Crises*, vol.2, no.2, 1978.
91. H. Fielding, *An Enquiry into the Causes of the Late Increase of Robbers* (Millar, 1751), pp. xv, 12; G. Rude, *Paris and London in the Eighteenth Century* (Fontana, 1970); S.R. Smith, 'The London Apprentices as Seventeenth Century Adolescents', *Past and Present*, no.61, 1973; Pearson, *Hooligan*, op. cit., pp. 187–8, 190–4.
92. M.G. Maxfield, *Fear of Crime in England and Wales*, Home Office Research Study no.78 (HMSO, 1984); M. Hough and P. Mayhew, *The British Crime Survey: First Report*, Home Office Research Study no.76 (HMSO, 1983); M. Hough and P. Mayhew, *Taking Account of Crime: Key Findings from the 1984 British Crime Survey*, Home Office Research Study no.85 (HMSO, 1985).
93. Hough and Mayhew, *Taking Account of Crime*, op. cit., pp.35–9.
94. Maxfield, *Fear of Crime*, op. cit., p. 1.
95. R. Kinsey, *Merseyside Crime Survey: First Report* (Merseyside County Council, 1984); B. MacLean, T. Jones and J. Young, *Preliminary Report of the Islington Crime Survey* (Centre for Criminology, Middlesex Polytechnic, 1986).
96. T. Jones and J. Young, 'Crime, Police and People', *New Society*, 24 Jan. 1986.
97. *Faith in the City: The Report of the Archbishop of Canterbury's Commission on Urban Priority Areas* (Church House Publishing, 1985). On anti-urban sentiments, see M.J. Wiener, *English Culture and the Decline of the Industrial Spirit, 1850–1980* (Cambridge University Press, 1981).

# CHAPTER THREE

# VIOLENCE IN THE HOME

## Jane Moonman*

### THE BACKGROUND

He ran a knife down my face just to show me where he was going to do it. Then he went out drinking. He was always drinking and coming back and urinating in the bed or the laundry basket and all over the floor. Next day he wouldn't believe he did it and would call me a slut and a liar and tell me to get out of the house and take that bastard (our little boy) with me.

The woman who wrote this was not living in poverty in Victorian England but in the relative prosperity of the late twentieth century in a council home in Pitsea, Essex. She was 26 years old, had married a man she had known for less than six months when she was 21 and had one child aged three. There are ways in which she is typical of today's victims of domestic violence. Both she and her husband had left school without qualifications and he had undergone long periods of unemployment. He had a serious drink problem and had been in trouble with the police for other criminal offences apart from beating his wife. Both husband and wife come from very large families where the father beat the mother, where there was a history of mental illness and alcoholism and where inter-relationships between and within the families were described as bad or non-existent. Neither the husband nor wife claimed to have friends and they had no interests in common. Violence was a regular part of this

*Jane Moonman has been a committee member and Trustee of the Basildon Emergency Accommodation Project since its inception in 1977. The Project runs a refuge for battered women and their children in Laindon, Essex. From 1979 to 1985, Mrs. Moonman carried out a survey among selected victims of violence at the refuge, to find out about the backgrounds of the women and their partners and whether any trends could be discerned.

marriage, a marriage which seemed to have no chance of success from the beginning.

Not all battered women answer the description of this one whom I shall call Susan, but a large number of them would find much that is familiar in her story.

Not much is known about marital violence of the kind that is 'frequent battering, calculated mental cruelty and repression'.[1] Most of it is committed by the man against the woman but there is some evidence of violent women and rather more of women who might be called prone to violence, that is who seem to stimulate a violent response from the people who share their lives. But most violence against wives, which includes assault and rape, appears to be unrelated to the behaviour of the woman. The Women's National Commission report on domestic violence[2] said,

> While research shows that such factors as over-crowded accommodation, coping with young children (especially more than one), unemployment and drunkenness may make violence more likely, the theory which best accords with the objective data is that wife battering is chiefly related to the personality and attitudes of violent men.

It is claimed by some researchers that only about 2 per cent of incidents of domestic violence are reported to the police. This would account for the lack of reliable evidence on why it occurs and the kind of people that are involved. However, in their analysis of police records for Glasgow and Edinburgh, Dr. Russell P. Dobash and Dr. R. Emerson Dobash (1980)[3] provided evidence that the second most common form of violence *reported to the police* in those cities was wife-battering, accounting for some 25 per cent of all recorded crime. If this represents only a tiny proportion of the amount of domestic violence which is actually committed, we have some idea of the size of the problem.

Many women suffer violence at home over many years before doing anything about it.[4] In the study referred to here, it was said that 62 per cent of the women questioned had been regularly beaten over a period of three years or more. The reasons they gave for submitting to it implied various forms of dependency as well as the shame of public exposure and fear of increased and worse attacks.

The Home Office have only once, in 1979, published figures for serious offences against spouses. The statistics have not been repeated because it was said that they were unreliable since so many cases go unreported. However, there are some published figures apart from those mentioned above which are helpful. The Home Office Judicial Statistics which record proceedings in the County Courts under the Domestic Violence and Matrimonial Proceedings Act 1976, the Home Office statistical bulletin which records proceedings in the Magistrates' Courts under the Domestic Violence and Magistrates' Courts Act of 1978 and the Metropolitan Commissioners Report on crimes of violence, all contain material which is relevant to the subject of domestic violence. We learn, for instance, that in 1982 104 women were murdered by their husband or lover and 12 men were murdered by their wife or lover. In 1984 there were 15,619 injunctions granted in England and Wales, about one third of them with powers of arrest. These injunctions prohibit men from committing acts of violence against their partners and/or their children. In the same year, there were 5,800 applications to Magistrates' Courts for exclusion orders prohibiting men from entering the matrimonial home and for non-molestation or protection orders. Of these, 48 per cent were actually granted. Further, the Metropolitan Commissioner's Report shows that people are almost as likely to be attacked by someone they know, including a member of the family, as by a stranger.

The Metropolitan Police records for 1979–84 show a 22% increase in violence against females, a 48% increase in rape and a 96% increase in robbery (theft involving a weapon) from a woman. Table 1 demonstrates particularly the increase in reported incidents of rape in the years 1973–84. There has, of course been an increase in all kinds of violence during the same period.

The first rape crisis centre opened in London in 1970 and there are now 45 over the whole country with plans to open more during the current year (1986). About 30 new cases are reported to the police each week but some researchers claim that 11 out of 12 cases remain unreported. In 1985 reported rape cases increased by 29% over the previous year.[5] It is said that the crime of rape is also getting 'nastier'; 50% of rape victims know their

TABLE 1: OFFENCES OF HOMICIDE WITH FEMALE VICTIMS AND RAPE RECORDED
BY THE POLICE IN ENGLAND AND WALES

| | Homicide | | | | Rape |
|---|---|---|---|---|---|
| | Victim aged under 1 | 1 – 15 | 16 and over | Total | |
| 1973 | 6 | 26 | 170 | 202 | 998 |
| 1974 | 22 | 32 | 182 | 236 | 1,052 |
| 1975 | 17 | 22 | 160 | 199 | 1,040 |
| 1976 | 18 | 26 | 195 | 239 | 1,094 |
| 1977 | 8 | 26 | 175 | 209 | 1,015 |
| 1978 | 12 | 22 | 168 | 202 | 1,243 |
| 1979 | 15 | 31 | 219 | 265 | 1,170 |
| 1980 | 17 | 20 | 227 | 264 | 1,225 |
| 1981 | 11 | 30 | 200 | 241 | 1,068 |
| 1982 | 16 | 33 | 209 | 258 | 1,336 |
| 1983 | 9 | 25 | 194 | 228 | 1,334 |
| 1984 | 7 | 34 | 203 | 244 | 1,443 |

*Source:* Criminal Statistics, England & Wales 1984, Tables 2.9, 4.6 and equivalent tables in
earlier editions.

rapist and most rapes occur in the woman's own home.

This scant statistical evidence gives some idea of the degree of
violence to which women are subjected by those with whom they
share their lives.

## REFUGES FOR BATTERED WOMEN AND THEIR
## CHILDREN

The problem was brought into prominence by the establishment in
the 1970s of a number of refuges for battered women and their
children. The best known campaigner was Erin Pizzey who set up a
refuge in Chiswick under the auspices of Women's Aid. All
involved in the problem today acknowledge that greater public
awareness and action has followed the dramatically demonstrated
need for the refuges after these early experiments were carried
out. The law has given women rights within marriage for many
years, but even articulate women find it difficult to assert those
rights in a relationship which is violent and which involves a strong
element of dependency by the woman on the man. The refuges
have acted as shelters and havens at the same time as providing the
women concerned with advice on how to pursue their rights, and
restoring sufficient confidence to them to allow them to accept the

idea that they can manage without the support of a violent husband.

Traditional attitudes displayed by both police and social workers have down-graded domestic violence to the level of 'what goes on between man and wife is nobody else's business' and 'these women ask for it'. It is only in relatively recent times that assaults against a wife have been viewed with the same degree of seriousness as an assault on a member of the public. It is true that when police attend the scene of a domestic dispute the woman who has been battered is frequently so terrified that she appears unreasonable and hysterical and may give an entirely wrong impression, to those who might otherwise help her, of the facts of her situation. Here again, refuge staff who are experienced in this area have been of immense assistance in changing the views of both police and public. A House of Commons Select Committee on Violence in Marriage which reported in 1975 recommended that there be one refuge per 10,000 population. Not only has this recommendation never been implemented but the money to maintain those refuges which were set up has not always been forthcoming and, with the withdrawal of Urban Aid, has been further decreased. Recognising the contribution made by Women's Aid to awareness of the extent and gravity of the problem of domestic violence, the Women's National Commission on Violence against Women[6] took evidence from Welsh Women's Aid which has been involved in providing refuge places for women and children in Wales for the past ten years. Their representative reported that

> in Wales . . . 25 refuges now offer accommodation, support and advice to over 1,000 women and up to twice as many children. This [situation] is reflected throughout Britain. The opening of Women's Aid refuges has provided an important measure of violence against women in the home. As each refuge has opened, women and children have sought protection and in Wales there is very rarely a vacant place at a refuge. Though there are now approximately 125 family places in Wales, the Select Committee's estimate would require us to have over 200 more places and we still believe that it would be insufficient for the demand both visible and hidden.

BASILDON EMERGENCY ACCOMMODATION PROJECT

The Welsh experience is borne out by all the established refuges in Great Britain. Susan, the battered wife from whom I quoted at the beginning of this essay, was a resident with her child at a refuge in Laindon, Essex, run by the Basildon Emergency Accommodation Project (BEAP). From the time that the refuge was opened in February 1977, the demand for the service it provides has far exceeded the supply. The maximum this small house can accommodate is about 80 women and 140 children per annum.

After several years of planning, false starts and opposition from prospective neighbours, the Basildon refuge was finally started courtesy of Basildon Development Corporation. It was a dwelling of the semi-detached variety with three bedrooms, a lounge and a sitting-room (which has consistently been used as a fourth bedroom) and a bathroom, with small gardens at the back and front. In the beginning, the project had no paid staff. It was run entirely by volunteers on money collected from each family usually out of social security payments. Out of this, rent had to be paid to the Corporation and food and other services had to be provided for the women and children in the refuge. In 1977, that was the sole regular source of income for the refuge.

The refuge was opened mainly as a result of the persistence of one or two local people, in particular a young woman who had herself been a battered wife and who later became the refuge's superintendent. During the first year, 78 women and 122 children were received at the refuge. In addition, there were about 50 referrals which had, for various reasons, to be sent elsewhere after being given temporary shelter. All the women and many of the children who have been through the refuge since its opening are battered, some severely, either mentally or physically. Some women come to the refuge having left children at home but the great majority bring an average of two to three children ranging in age from one to seven years old with them.

The families are allocated a room in which they must all sleep, while the lounge, kitchen, bathroom and gardens are communal. Each family stays an average of three months but some have been in the refuge for seven months or even longer. The organisers must respect the Basildon Development Corporation's 'no overcrowding' requirement while maintaining an open-door policy for overnight emergencies. Any families in excess of four have to be referred to other refuges in the locality the following day.

While they are in the refuge, the organisers try to assist families with re-housing, with court applications for divorce, separation or injunctions, often attending court with the women in order to provide moral support; children are placed in local schools or play-groups and the families are put in touch with the local Social Services to arrange benefits, with local doctors and with the Job Centre for those who require a job. The refuge therefore genuinely provides emergency accommodation while the multiple problems of the battered women and their children are sorted out. The organisers of the refuge have to ensure that the house is kept clean and tidy as well as undertaking all the support roles described above, being on call literally 24 hours a day and coping with enraged husbands who may present themselves at unsociable hours.

Most referrals come from local Social Services or council agencies, from the Samaritans, the police, the local hospital almoner and from other refuges.

From the money paid by each family every week, the project pays the rent of the house, lighting, gas, telephone and television licence and rental. If the house is full, the books just about balance. Each family is responsible for buying its own food and it also pays a small amount of money each week towards the cost of cleaning materials for the house. Each family must also provide clothing for themselves and their children. The project is responsible for raising money for repairs to the house, for decorations and improvements and for the upkeep of the gardens. The project has always had very good professional support from local Social Services, schools and play-groups. It has a management committee which discusses individual cases and is responsible for fund-raising. In 1980, the project became a registered charity and at various stages in its history has attracted grants from the Manpower Commission, the Essex County Council and from Basildon Council. Voluntary fund-raising has been sporadic but extremely necessary, particularly since, in recent years, the project has had to pay the supervisors of the refuge who were unable to continue on a permanently voluntary basis. Nevertheless, volunteers still play an important role as does the generosity of local people and industry who respond to appeals in the Basildon newspapers.

Despite the various grants and individual generosity, the refuge continues to exist precariously and it is obvious even on a first visit that it is a home of poverty. A 'second stage' home was opened in 1983 to receive families needing longer-term support and this is run on the same lines as the original refuge and with precisely the same financial difficulties.

Nevertheless, those involved in the project have never at any time doubted the need for it.


THE SURVEY

In 1978, after interviewing women at the refuge, one of whom had been branded by her husband with a red hot poker and another who had been made to crawl on all fours in front of her children and bark like a dog, I decided that those involved in running the project should attempt some kind of rudimentary research into the backgrounds of both the women and their partners so that we could reach a better understanding of why the phenomenon of domestic violence occurs and what circumstances lead to it. I began by interviewing a girl whom I shall call Mary referred to me by the project supervisor as somebody who was not only willing but actually needed to talk about her experience. She had been raped by her father when she was ten years old and she had frequently witnessed her father beating her mother. At 15, she was put by her father on the streets to earn money as a prostitute and to escape from this she married at 18 a boy who already had a police record. He began beating her from the moment they were married and he, in turn, forced her to continue earning money as a prostitute in order to keep him. She arrived in the refuge aged 22 with two children after her husband had been arrested. He was later sent to prison for assault on his wife and for other criminal activities. While she was at the Basildon refuge, she petitioned for divorce and was re-housed with her two children.

Not many of the case studies are as horrific as Mary's but, after interviewing women who came to the refuge during the whole of 1978, I decided that we should attempt to tabulate their experiences in a more organised way. We agreed upon the questionnaire method as being the best way to collate the information which was available to us. In consultation with the then superintendent of the Basildon refuge and with some of the more interested and articulate of the victims of violence who came to the refuge, a lengthy and detailed questionnaire was finally drawn up. It was used to conduct a limited pilot survey in order to establish the questions that needed re-phrasing, those which needed to be asked but which had been omitted and those which were unlikely to produce fruitful answers. Some of the questions (the questionnaire is produced in the Appendix) e.g. those relating to other symptoms of tension such as nail-biting and smoking, and those concerning the friendships of husband and wife, were included as a direct result of remarks made to me by residents at the refuge, some of whom had discussed domestic violence with many other victims. I wanted to go into the background of both marriage partners to try to shed some light on why it is that some people believe that violence is a legitimate outlet for frustration and an acceptable element in marriage. It is those questions rather than those which relate to the personal details of the battered women which have, in my view, produced the most interesting answers.

Although we carried on the survey over a period of six years, it produced only 60 usable answers. The sample is therefore very small, currently too small to enable us to draw concrete conclusions. However, the questionnaire was so full and so detailed and some of the women who responded were so fluent that the amount of data available to us was greater than a sample of 60 would suggest. There were a total of 70 questions relating to the personal details, the education, religion, childhood background, inter-family relationships, the relationship between husband and wife, the children of the family, the help which the wife had sought, the role of the refuge and finally, question 70 was an open-ended invitation to the battered woman to explain her own thoughts and feelings on her predicament. Only those women who were interested in the research we were carrying out and who felt that they wanted to talk about their situation were invited to complete the questionnaire. The Refuge supervisor sometimes completed the questionnaire on behalf of the woman as she spoke.

## Results

Much of what we have learned is not new but I believe that some of it is and, in an area where so little research has been done, the information we have collected makes a contribution, however modest, to our understanding of the phenomenon of domestic violence. At the very least, a certain similarity or pattern can be discerned in the responses which provides pointers to back up what we already know or to indicate areas which require more systematic research. The most significant results of this survey of 60 battered women are as follows (figures have been rounded to the nearest whole percentage):

– most (55%) of the relationships started when the woman was under 20 years old,
– a large proportion (43%) of the relationships started after less than 12 months from first meeting,
– the overwhelming majority of both men (82%) and women (83%) left school before the age of 16,
– most of the men (88%) and the women (71%) left school with no qualifications,
– 75% of the men were or had been unemployed,
– 43% of the men had a drink or drug problem,
– 68% of the men had been in trouble with the police for reasons other than domestic violence,
– 38% of the men and 23% of the women came from families with more than 5 children,
– 35% of the men were the oldest child in their family,
– 35% of the women and 25% of the men had parents who were divorced,
– 33% of the women's and 56% of the men's fathers beat their mothers.
– In 47% of cases there was violence among other members of the men's families.
– In 39% of cases there had been mental illness among either or

both families.
- In 43% of cases there were drink or drug problems in either or both families.
- In 91% of cases there was no inter-relationship between the two families.
- In 97% of cases children had witnessed violence between their parents.
- In 75% of cases the partners had no shared interests.
- 92% of the males had no friends according to their wives.
- In 73% of cases there were no mutual friends between the partners.
- 78% of the women had been to the police before finally going to the refuge.
- 64% of the women knew other battered wives apart from those they had met at the refuge.

These results amount to a picture of ill-preparedness for life, let alone for marriage. They tell a story of inadequacy, inability to relate to others and lack of support outside the institutionalised systems. Perhaps the most interesting and even original finding is the high proportion of both men and women in violent partnerships who come from very large families. Some of these families had as many as 14 or even 19 children. Alongside an absence of friendship and violence within the marriage, this finding may be a pointer to serious study of the effects of being a member of a large family and the ability to form stable relationships. It is an observable fact that tensions occur in all families. In families where there are a large number of children, the chances of material and emotional deprivation must increase alongside the intensity of inter-familial tensions.

A more detailed analysis of the answers to the questionnaire, item-by-item, follows.

## Age
46 or 76.7% of the 60 women in the survey were aged between 20 and 40 years old and most of these were in the age group 25–35. These are, of course, the years in which women who have children and no means of earning a living are at their most dependent. There were five women (8.3%) under the age of 20,

all but one with young children, and one aged 77 who was said by
the refuge workers to be the worst case of battering they had ever
had. This lady said in answer to question 70 at the end of the
questionnaire that she could not remember much about the early
days of her marriage or anything at all about her husband's
family. She knew the violence started soon after she was married
and had continued at regular intervals throughout. She had never
sought help or left home before though one of her two children
left at an early age because he could not tolerate the violence any
longer. She had become resigned to the beatings being a part of
her relationship with her husband and it was only after reading
about the Basildon refuge in the local paper and after a particularly vicious attack by her husband that she had finally made the
break. She had no regrets but feared being placed in an old age
home. Another woman of 52 who had suffered beatings over a
period of 22 years told how, apart from hitting her, her husband
had battered her mentally and robbed her of confidence. She
wrote:

> I am afraid of my husband and do not want to go back to him.
> He always complains that I watch too much television and
> he keeps telling me that I should not have my light on as he
> pays the bills. . . . I kept crying for help of somebody but
> not knowing anybody I did not know which way to turn . . .
> I hope that when all this is over, I would like to find a job and
> make a new life for myself, then I'll know I'm not having my
> husband looking over my shoulder and keep saying horrible
> things to me. I know he thinks I loved my son more than him
> but that was not true. But now I know after all it was true
> because of the way he has treated me.

### Geographical origins

The great majority of women in the refuge had come from the
Basildon and surrounding districts to the refuge (38.3% from
Basildon and 36.7% from elsewhere in Essex). 18.3% came from
districts in London and 6.7% from other places such as
Birmingham and Wales. One woman had thumbed a lift from a
lorry driver in Scotland and had landed in Basildon because that
is where he happened to be going. By contrast, most of the

women and their husbands had been born outside Essex, 46% of them not even in the London area. They had come from places as far apart as Ireland, Karachi, Guyana and Trinidad. As Basildon is a new town, developed in the post-World War II period, and Essex generally has attracted population from London during the same years, this is not so surprising. 50% of the men and 46% of the women involved were born outside Essex and Greater London. What this means in real terms is that the couples were generally living some distance away from their own families which could not, therefore, offer a supporting role.

## Housing

The majority of the women (51.7%) who came to the refuge lived in council or corporation housing though more than a quarter were buying their own homes. Basildon and its surrounding neighbourhoods, Laindon and Pitsea, have large estates of new town development corporation and local council housing with a growing private sector. There is very little privately rented property available. These factors are reflected in the housing situation of the women who come to the refuge, though it is perhaps surprising that more than 26.7% are upwardly mobile and were living in homes which the family were in the process of buying.

## Age on marriage and length of relationship before marriage

55% of the women were under 20 when they married or started to co-habit, and a further 26.7% were aged between 20 and 25; 11.7% were between 25 and 30 and only 6.6% were over the age of 30. The majority of the women were therefore very young when they set up home with their violent partner. 22.4% of the women in this survey knew their partners for less than six months before setting up home with them and a further 20.7% had known them for between 6 and 12 months. Rather more, 37.9% said that they had known their partners for between one and two years.

## Children

Almost all the couples in the survey had children, most of them very young. 28.3% had one child, 36.7% had two and 31.7% had three children. The dependency of children was frequently advanced as a reason for tolerating violence and also as the main reason why the woman finally left home taking the children with her. The women generally wanted to provide a more secure and stable environment for their children and were afraid of the effects of constant aggression on the children's own behaviour. When asked about their plans for the future, the women would often express a wish to start a new life, especially for their children. Question 67 (see Appendix) asked the women about their current anxieties and these also frequently centred on fear of losing children to local authorities or of not being able to provide for them on their own.

**Religion**

The biggest group of women in religious terms were those who claimed to be Church of England (43.1%) and the second largest group were those who had no religion at all (36.2%). 12% were Catholic and 8.7% came from other religious groupings. Again, this is not a surprising finding in the context of Basildon and surrounding districts where there is only a small immigrant population and few places of worship outside the mainstream. There were among the women with allegiance to other religions, two Moslems, a Sikh and a woman married to a Jewish husband. One of the Moslem women came from Turkey and her husband, also a Moslem, from Cyprus. This woman was unusual in that she had stayed in full-time education until the age of 18 and had ambitions to go to art school once her domestic problems were sorted out. Her parents were divorced and her father, who was an alcoholic, had beat her mother. Her greatest regret was that she had had children when she was quite young, which had prevented her from abandoning her marriage until the time she went to the refuge. Unusually, a Sikh woman, whose husband was also a Sikh, both born in India, presented herself at the refuge with her three young children during 1983. Leaving aside her religion and national origin, her problems were very much the same as those of the average battered wife. Her husband had a severe drink problem as had his father. In fact, alcoholism seemed to run in the husband's family. She had received severe head injuries during beatings from her husband as well as stomach injuries which had twice caused her to be hospitalised. She said, during her interview with the refuge supervisor,

My marriage was an arranged one. Obviously my parents did not know about his family. His mother was a wicked woman and I just couldn't get on with her and she expected too much from me being an Indian daughter-in-law, whereas she allowed her son to go out with other men drinking. When I begged him not to come home drunk he said to me all the time 'I will do what I want to do'. He made me so uncomfortable to live with him because he started to say that he would kill me and the children . . . at the end, he did set fire to my house and burned it knowing that myself and the children were inside and now at the moment, he is held in prison for the hearing.

## Education

The majority of the men (82.3%) and women (83.4%) had left school by the age of 16. Very few (2% of the men and 3.3% of the women) went on to higher education over the age of 18. Most of the people involved in the partnerships in this survey therefore left school with no qualifications (71.4% of the women and 87.7% of the men). There were no university graduates in this particular survey, though some respondents had some O levels or CSEs. In general, such qualifications as were held were of the practical (secretarial, plumbing, nursing) rather than the academic kind. One couple, both of whom came from Ghana, had received full-time education well into adulthood. The husband worked as a bank executive and, unlike most of the men in the survey, had never been unemployed. He came from a family of nine children; his wife was one of 11. Both his father and his brother were said to be wife-beaters. The wife, who was in the refuge, had suffered bruises, black eyes and cuts to her head and all three children of the family displayed signs of anxiety and aggressive behaviour.

## Employment

Most of the women in the survey (96.7%) had worked at some

stage in their lives, about half of them in skilled work such as hairdressing, secretarial employment and nursing. The remainder had done casual, unskilled work in factories and shops or as cleaners. More than half the men (53.6%) worked or had worked in skilled trades such as tiling, joinery or driving. 21.4% did unskilled work as caretakers, refuse collectors and labourers for instance. 10.7% were professional (one was a Merchant Navy officer, one an executive director and one a social worker, for example) and as many had never been employed at all. 75% of the men in the survey were or had been unemployed during their marriage.

The woman who was married to a Merchant Navy officer was 49 years old when she arrived at the refuge. She had five children ranging in ages from 14 to 21 and had left school at age 16 with five school certificate passes. Both husband and wife were born in Ireland, were raised as Catholics and came from very large families. The husband was a heavy drinker. This woman said when completing the questionnaire:

> What I found very hard was to see my husband smash all the things I worked and saved so hard to get, while he drank and gambled his money away. What he did not smash he took and sold for drink. The nights were the worst. When he came back from the pub everyone would run to bed. . . . The police were no help, especially one policeman who told me he could smash the place up and threaten me as much as he liked while he was married to me. If it wasn't for my two younger boys, I think I would have jumped in the river, but they talked to me and kept me going.

The husband who was a social worker was born in Karachi, India. Both the husband and his wife, who was a nurse, came from broken homes. There were three teenaged children, all girls, in this family, two of whom the mother had to leave at home when she went to the refuge. This was her biggest anxiety while she remained in the refuge. She said:

> I met my husband when I was 16 years old. I thought I knew everything until I gave birth to my first baby nine months later, then I realized I knew very little of life. My husband

showed signs of violence after the birth of my first baby. I could always find an excuse for him. He had been married before so that was the main excuse plus the fact that I was so inadequate as a mother. . . . My husband has completely dominated me, so much so I feel I have no real personality left at all. I think my confidence in myself will probably return in time but never to the extent I had before meeting my husband. That part of me has died. I now feel like an empty shell. Not much good for anything or anybody.

This reaction is common among women who come to the refuge. It was echoed by another nurse who arrived at the refuge with teenaged children. 'I loved my husband very much. It seemed that I could not please him but being here I have found out that his other wife was treated in the same way. I always thought I lacked something.'

In this case both partners were born locally and were living in Pitsea. Again, the husband was a drinker but in this case it was the woman who came from a violent home. She had been beaten more than 12 times in one year and had suffered a broken jaw, a bruised head, cracked ribs, a broken nose and her husband had attempted to strangle her.

## Drink, drugs, cigarettes, nail-biting, crime

None of the women admitted to having a drink or drug problem but 43.3% of them said their husbands did. In most cases it was said to be serious and to be a contributory factor to violence in the home. 78.3% of the women smoked and 40% had a nail-biting habit. 20% of the women admitted to having been in trouble with the police while 68.3% of the men had criminal records. The respondents to the survey were not asked to specify for what reasons they or their husbands had been in trouble but some volunteered the information. In the small number of cases involving the women, they had convictions for shop-lifting or soliciting. The men had been convicted for drink-related crimes such as driving while unfit and indecent exposure as well as theft, actual bodily harm, common assault, criminal damage and disturbances of the peace.

Almost all the women (90%) said that they liked running a home and carrying out domestic chores.

## Family size

78.3% of the women in this survey came from families where there were three or more children; in 23.3% of them there were more than five children in the family. The proportion of husbands who came from larger families was even more startling. In 81.7% there were three or more children and in 38.4% there were more than five. In the case of both men and women, more were the eldest of the family (women 33.4%; men 35%) than in any other position among siblings. Next came the second position in the family (30% of the women; 20% of the men) and then third or youngest of the family (10% of the women; 18.3% of the men). This finding is consistent with an assumption of greater stress and responsibility being placed on older children in large families.

The largest family in the survey was that of a man who was the youngest of 19. He was his wife's third husband (her second husband had also been violent) and they had married after knowing one another for only two months. Both were born in Dublin and were practising Catholics. The man was said by his wife to be an alcoholic who had not worked in many years. They had two young children, both in care. Their families had never met and the husband had no contact with his own family and no friends. His father had beat his mother and all his brothers were violent to their families. He beat his own wife at least three times a week and she had left home on twelve previous occasions to go to the police or to other refuges. Her main anxiety while she was in the Basildon refuge was the fact that she was unable to have her children with her.

## Family backgrounds

Most of the people in the survey had one or both parents still alive and most of the surviving parent couples remained married. 35% of the women's parents were divorced or separated and 25% of the men's. Only 5% in each case had never married.

33.3% of the women and 55.6% of the men came from homes where the father beat the mother and 46.7% of the women claimed that there was violence among other members of their husbands' families. Many fewer (18.6%) said there was violence going on in their own families.

As many as 38.6% of the women claimed there was 'mental illness' in the broader family, though they were not asked to define what they meant by this term. 42% of them said there were drink or drug problems in the wider families. More than half the women (52.7%) said they either had no relationship at all with their in-laws or that relationships were bad, 14.6% described them as 'okay' and 32.7% as 'good'. In the overall majority of cases (87.3%) there was no support for the woman forthcoming from her in-laws. Relationships between the men and their own parents were estimated by their partners to be 'bad' in 46.3% of cases, 'okay' in 22.2% and 'good' in 31.5%. Between them and the woman's parents, relationships were said to be better ('good' 41.5%, 'okay' 26.4%, 'bad' 32.1%) and between the woman and *her* parents a little more so ('good' 50.9%, 'okay' 17% and 'bad' 32.1%). There was barely any relationship at all between the two families concerned in the partnerships.

## The violence

The women in this survey were beaten anything from three times during the marriage to daily. They made comments like 'I was beaten too often to remember' or 'I lost count of the beatings' and 'I was beaten all through the marriage'. The injuries they sustained were mainly consistent with punches from a bare fist (black eyes, bruises, perforated ear-drums, broken noses and cut lips) but some were the result of weapons being used or of being kicked (cracked skull, burn marks, torn ear-lobe, cuts from a leather belt, knife wounds) and some were sexual attacks (rape, blows to the abdomen causing miscarriage, instruments pushed in the vagina).

Rows leading to violence could start from almost anything but drunkenness was quoted as a frequent cause. Jealousy (usually sexual jealousy),[7] children, money matters, depression and even television programmes could lead to a fight. 71.6% of the women had left home before the occasion on which they went to the Basildon refuge, usually two or three times but occasionally as many as 15 or 16 times.

In 96.5% of cases where there were children of the family, they had witnessed the violence between husband and wife resulting, at least in the opinion of their mothers, in distress symptoms such as bed-wetting, vomiting, poor sleep patterns, expressions of fear, speech defects, aggression and poor performance in school. Rather more of the fathers (51%) were not violent towards their children than were but those that were had sometimes caused severe damage to young children. One father broke his small daughter's arm in two places, one fractured a baby's skull and broke his leg (the child was taken into care; the father was a drug addict with a drink problem) and another bit his five-year-old son all down his body.

Just under half (48.9%) of the children were aggressive to others or to their mothers. This was something the refuge were in a good position to judge as some of the children there were difficult to contain.

### General relationship between the partners

Most of the men (70%) were said by the women to have shown remorse for their violence on at least some occasions but the shame was usually short-lived. 45% of the women said that the sexual relationship between them and their partner was satisfactory. Of the 55% who said it was not, several said it 'used to be' or 'it was in the beginning' but the violence had put them off sex altogether or drink had made the intimate part of the relationship 'mechanical' or 'horrible'. One woman said her husband had raped her and thereafter she feared sex.

75% of the couples had no shared interests and almost as many (73.3%) had no shared friends. Most of the women in the survey and almost all the men had no 'special' or 'best' friend. The women sometimes named a female relative or someone at the refuge as their closest friend but the men were largely loners, occasionally having drinking mates whom they barely knew away from the pub.

### Action taken by the women

Predictably, most of the women (68%) had no life of their own, hobbies or outside interests, sometimes saying their husbands would not permit it. Some, however, did go to bingo or to keep-fit classes or to discos, some did needlework or knitting and one said that she did voluntary work while another had taken up cookery classes.

All the women had sought help before going to the Basildon refuge, some of them from more than one agency. 48.3% said they had been to other refuges, 23.3% to the police, 45% to the Citizens' Advice Bureau, the National Society for the Prevention of Cruelty to Children, the Yoyo Group (a group in Basildon dealing with children of separated parents), or health visitors and 68.3% said they had been to a solicitor, to the Marriage Guidance Council, to a probation officer, their doctor, the Samaritans or to various relatives.

71.7% of them had been to court because of their partners' violence, usually resulting in an injunction against them not to enter the matrimonial home or not to molest their wife and children. 23.3% of the women who went to the police said they were unhelpful or even disinterested.

Only one woman in the whole survey regretted going to the refuge. 98.3% felt the refuge had been an enormous help to them but as the women were completing the questionnaires while they were in the refuge, their responses on this question cannot be said to be 'free'. However, almost all of them did credit the refuge with having given them protection, shelter, company, security, sympathy, advice and confidence. It would probably be fair to say that the women refrained from negative comment on this question.

83.3% of the women said they had plans for the future, including plans to divorce or legally separate. Many wanted to get a job or to undertake some kind of educational training – more had ambitions centred on their children for whom they wished to make a 'nice and happy home'. One woman, who had left school at 15 with no qualifications, had become interested in domestic law during her many visits to solicitors, police and courts and had decided she wanted to try to get to law school. She said in answer to her questionnaire:

> Although my husband has never been a high wage-earner, as he is unskilled, I found he had no ambitions or interests

apart from gambling and drinking in the pub. I myself feel ambitious and would very much like to have a secure career. . . . I would like to think my husband would seek help for his condition but I can never see this materialising as he seems to see nothing wrong with the way he is. I no longer care for my husband so for my children and my own sake I see no solution but divorce.

Asked about their anxieties, the women responded variously but many were very insecure, doubting their ability to maintain their children or to cope generally, fearing loneliness and their husbands' continued dominance of their lives.

64% of the women knew other battered wives apart from those they had met at the refuge, an indication of how prevalent the problem of domestic violence is.


CONCLUSIONS

It would be unwise to draw any general conclusions from a small sample of 60 women from one refuge. The circumstances at the refuge in Basildon are, to some extent, a product of the environment in which the refuge is placed. For instance, Basildon is a new town with a larger than average proportion of council and corporation-owned property. Again, because it is a new town, the families tend to be at most second generation but many of them are first generation in the district. The social isolation is probably above average therefore. These and other circumstantial factors must be taken into account when assessing the results of this survey. It cannot be concluded, for instance, that academics do not beat their wives because no wife of a graduate husband had found her way to the Basildon refuge. It is known that domestic violence occurs across the social spectrum, but fewer cases are recorded in the higher socio-economic groupings. This may be because other solutions than flight to a refuge are available to the wives in those groupings. Or it may be that the conditions that this survey suggests are most likely to produce domestic violence, occur more frequently at the lower socio-economic levels.

However, the survey in the Basildon refuge produced results

which are sufficiently in line with the little that is known about domestic violence across the country to permit some tentative conclusions. Thus, it would seem that wife-battering is more likely to occur in economically deprived or unstable households. Some of the contributory factors seem to be – unemployment, alcoholism, family backgrounds which include large numbers of children and violence between parents, social isolation and low attainment levels.

A firmer conclusion which can be drawn is that the refuges which have been established for some time in the United Kingdom are under-used as potential sources of research. The resources allocated to the provision of refuges and their successful maintenance are so inadequate that research seems a luxury. However, it is certain that if anything is ever to be done about reducing the level of domestic violence, a good deal more needs to be known about it.

Fortunately, both the public and the police are becoming increasingly aware of the extent and nature of violence against women. A new report on domestic violence and the police, which was commissioned by the Metropolitan Police will, if its recommendations are accepted, give greater help and protection to battered women. The report recommended that a pilot scheme first be introduced to improve police training for dealing with violence in the home and to give better support systems to the victims of this violence. Recommendations are made that more hostels and social service resources be devoted to the sheltering of battered women and their children and that there should be better record-keeping of incidents and a greater use of the Police and Criminal Evidence Act provisions to allow police to prosecute whether a battered wife agrees to go ahead with a prosecution or not. The enquiry was set up in the autumn of 1984 and reported at the end of 1985. The major breakthrough appears to be that at least the senior officials in the Police Force have accepted that an assault is an assault wherever it occurs and against whomsoever it is committed. A woman will no longer have to make the decision to prosecute on her own and may be less afraid to give evidence. Similar laws have been introduced in Ontario, Canada with good effect. There are now more prosecutions and fewer re-offending husbands as well as more wives appearing to give evidence. The first few months of 1986 saw increased media attention being paid to the escalating incidence of rape including rape within marriage. Commentators noted in particular the tendency towards the use of weapons and deviations during rape, and sentences for rapists were accordingly increased. The hand of those who want to reform attitudes on domestic violence has therefore been strengthened, in particular in the move to put more resources into the investigation of its causes. Wife-battering is as old as society. Perhaps the late 1980s will see it finally becoming totally unacceptable.

APPENDIX

Questionnaire and Statistical Summary of Answers
(in percentages)

The number of respondents was 60 in total. Where fewer than 60 women answered a question, this is indicated in brackets underneath the question.

1. **Date**

2. **Name**

3. **Single name, if married**

4. **Age**

| under 20 | 8.3 |
| 20–30 | 41.7 |
| 30–40 | 35 |
| 40–50 | 8.3 |
| 50+ | 6.7 |

5. **Last address**

| Basildon | 38.3 |
| Essex | 36.7 |
| London | 18.3 |
| Other | 6.7 |

6. **Where were you born?**

| Basildon area | 2 |
| Essex | 19 |
| London | 33 |

Other                    46
(out of 58)

7. **Where was your husband born?**

| Basildon | 5.2 |
| Essex | 15.5 |
| London | 29.3 |
| Other | 50 |

8. **Do you live in council property, privately rented, your own home, a squat?**

| Council/corporation | 61.7 |
| Own home | 26.7 |
| Privately rented | 8.3 |
| Other | 3.3 |

9. **How old were you when you got married or started to co-habit?**

| Under 20 | 55 |
| 20–25 | 26.7 |
| 25–30 | 11.7 |
| Over 30 | 6.6 |

10. **How long had you known your husband when you got married?**

| | |
|---|---|
| Under 6 months | 22.4 |
| 6–12 months | 20.7 |
| 1–2 years | 37.9 |
| Over 2 years | 19.0 |
| (out of 58) | |

11. **Names and ages of children**

| | |
|---|---|
| 1 | 28.3 |
| 2 | 36.7 |
| 3 | 31.7 |
| 5 | 3.3 |

12. **Do you have a religion?**

| | |
|---|---|
| C of E | 62.8 |
| RC | 15.2 |
| Other | 6.8 |
| None | 15.2 |
| (out of 59) | |

13. **Does your husband?**

| | |
|---|---|
| C of E | 43.1 |
| RC | 12 |
| Other | 8.7 |
| None | 36.2 |
| (out of 58) | |

14. **How old were you when you left full-time education?**

| | |
|---|---|
| Under 15 | 13.3 |
| 15–16 | 70.1 |
| 16–18 | 13.3 |
| Over 18 | 3.3 |

15. **How old was your husband when he left full-time education?**

| | |
|---|---|
| Under 15 | 19.6 |
| 15–16 | 62.7 |
| 16–18 | 15.7 |
| Over 18 | 2 |
| (out of 51) | |

16. **Did you get any certificates or other qualifications?**

| | |
|---|---|
| Yes | 28.6 |
| No | 71.4 |

17. **Did he?**

| | |
|---|---|
| Yes | 12.3 |
| No | 87.7 |
| (out of 57) | |

18. **Have you ever had a job?**

| | |
|---|---|
| Yes | 96.7 |
| No | 3.3 |
| (out of 58) | |

19. **If so, what?**

| | |
|---|---|
| Skilled | 48.3 |
| Unskilled | 48.3 |
| Professional | 3.4 |

20. **What is your husband's job?**

| | |
|---|---|
| Skilled | 53.6 |
| Unskilled | 21.4 |
| Professional | 10.7 |
| Retired | 1.8 |
| Self-employed | 1.8 |
| Never employed | 10.7 |
| (out of 56) | |

21. **Has he been unemployed?**

| | |
|---|---|
| Yes | 75 |
| No | 25 |

22. **Do you have a drink or a drug problem?**

| | |
|---|---|
| No | 100 |

23. **Does your husband?**

| | |
|---|---|
| Yes | 43.3 |
| No | 56.7 |

24. **Do you smoke?**

| | |
|---|---|
| Yes | 78.3 |
| No | 21.7 |

25. **Do you bite your nails?**

| | |
|---|---|
| Yes | 40 |
| No | 60 |

26. **Have you ever been in trouble with the police?**

| | |
|---|---|
| Yes | 20 |
| No | 80 |

27. **Has your husband?**

| | |
|---|---|
| Yes | 68.3 |
| No | 31.7 |

28. **Do you like running a house, cooking etc?**

| | |
|---|---|
| Yes | 90 |
| No | 10 |

29. **How many children were in your family at home?**

| | |
|---|---|
| 1 | 8.3 |
| 2 | 13.3 |
| 3 | 23.3 |
| 4 | 21.7 |
| 5 | 10 |
| More | 23.3 |

30. **Where did you come in the family?**

| | |
|---|---|
| 1 | 33.4 |
| 2 | 30 |
| 3 | 15 |
| 4 | 8.3 |
| 5 | 3.3 |
| 6+ | 10 |

31. **How many were in your husband's family?**

| | |
|---|---|
| 1 | 3.3 |
| 2 | 15 |
| 3 | 18.3 |
| 4 | 20 |
| 5 | 5 |
| More | 38.4 |

32. **Where did he come in his family?**

| | |
|---|---|
| 1 | 35 |
| 2 | 20 |
| 3 | 15 |

| | |
|---|---|
| 4 | 6.7 |
| 5 | 5 |
| 6+ | 18.3 |

33. **Are your parents alive?**

| | |
|---|---|
| Deceased | 20 |
| One or both alive | 80 |

34. **Are his?**

| | |
|---|---|
| Deceased | 18.3 |
| One or both alive | 81.7 |

35. **Are your parents separated or divorced?**

| | |
|---|---|
| Yes | 35 |
| No | 60 |
| Never married | 5 |

36. **Are his?**

| | |
|---|---|
| Yes | 25 |
| No | 70 |
| Never married | 5 |

37. **Did your father beat your mother ever?**

| | |
|---|---|
| Yes | 33.3 |
| No | 66.7 |
| (out of 54) | |

38. **As far as you know, did your husband's father beat his wife?**

| | |
|---|---|
| Yes | 55.6 |
| No | 44.4 |
| (out of 54) | |

39. **As far as you know, is there any violence going on among any other members of your or your husband's family?**

| | |
|---|---|
| Her | |
| Yes | 18.6 |
| No | 81.4 |
| (out of 43) | |
| Him | |
| Yes | 46.7 |

No 53.3
(out of 45)

40. **Do you know if there is or has been any mental illness in either family?**

Yes 38.6
No 61.4
(out of 57)

41. **Do you know if there is or has been any drink or drug problem in either family?**

Yes 42.9
No 57.1
(out of 56)

42. **How would you rate your relationship with your in-laws?**

Good 32.7
OK 14.5
Bad 32.7
Non-existent 20
(out of 55)

43. **Are they supportive to you?**

Yes 12.7
No 87.3
(out of 55)

44. **How would you rate your husband's relationship with his parents?**

Good 31.5
OK 22.2
Bad 46.3
(out of 54)

45. **How does your husband get on with your parents?**

Good 41.5
OK 26.4
Bad 32.1
(out of 53)

46. **How do you get on with your parents?**

Good 50.9
OK 17
Bad 32.1
(out of 53)

47. **How much inter-relationship is there between your two families? Describe the relationship**

Good 4.3
OK 4.3
Bad 91.4
(out of 48)

48. **How often have you been beaten by your husband?**

49. **What injuries have you sustained?**

50. **What generally would start a row leading to violence?**

51. **Have you left home before?**

Yes 71.6
No 28.4

52. **Have your children witnessed any violence?**

Yes 96.5
No 3.5
(out of 57)

53. **If so, how have they been affected?**

54. **Has your husband been violent with the children?**

Yes 49
No 51

55. **Are the children aggressive, violent to other children or to you?**

Yes                          48.9
No                           51.1
(out of 46)

56. **Has your husband ever shown any remorse for his actions?**

Yes                          70
No                           30

57. **Has the sexual relationship with your husband been satisfactory?**

Yes                          45
No                           55

58. **Have you and your husband any shared interests?**

Yes                          25
No                           75

59. **Do you have a best friend?**

No                           60.5
Female relative              15.8
Other                        23.7

60. **Who is your husband's best friend?**

No one                       92
Drinking mates               8

61. **Do you have mutual friends?**

Yes                          26.7
No                           73.3

62. **Do you have a 'life of your own' i.e. hobbies, activities not shared by your husband?**

Yes                          32
No                           68

63. **Which agencies or people have you been to for help?**

Other refuges                48.3
Police                       23.3
Social service institutions  45
Other                        68.3

64. **Have you been to the police/court?**

Yes                          71.7
No                           28.3

65. **Has the refuge been a support to you?**

Yes                          98.3
No                           1.7

66. **Have you any plans for the future?**

Yes                          83.3
No                           16.7

67. **What worries you most about your situation?**

68. **Do you know any other battered women apart from those at the refuge?**

Yes                          64
No                           36

69. **Would you mind if your name was given to researchers/ journalists/TV/provided it was not published?**

70. **Is there anything you would like to add or explain additional to the questionnaire?**

NOTES

1. 'Violence Against Women', Report of an Ad-Hoc Working Group, Women's National Commission, 1985.
2. Ibid.
3. Ibid.
4. Jan Pahl, ed., *Private Violence & Public Policy: The Needs of Battered Women and the Response of the Public Services*, Binney, Harkell & Nixon, 1985.
5. Home Office Statistical Bulletin, 1985.
6. Ibid.
7. Cf. Dobash and Dobash in *British Journal of Criminology*, Sept. 1984.

# CHAPTER FOUR

# STRESS AND THE INDIVIDUAL

## Jim Patten

In one of his essays, Hilaire Belloc describes a heavy field gun, discarded on the site of a battle, the obsolete relic of some earlier European war. On the gun are inscribed the words 'Ultima Ratio Regum', which may be translated as 'the last reason (or the last argument, or the last resort) of Kings'. Military violence is the method to which governments have resorted, in order to obtain their objectives, when all other methods have been unsuccessful, and in some cases even before that stage has been reached. For violence is often a form of problem-solving activity. In this respect, the governments of nations are no different from individual human beings, or indeed from animals, in using violence to satisfy a need or to solve a problem.

Seldom, if ever, is violence entirely without purpose, although the purpose might not be apparent to the observer, or to the victim, or even to the perpetrator. So what are the purposes which violence serves?

For the psychologist, the study of human violence must be part of the wider study of aggressive behaviour. Aggression, in terms of psychological theories of behaviour, has been well explored and documented over the past hundred years. While no explanation has proved entirely adequate, and some have only a limited application, they have made a contribution to our understanding of the issues. Detailed exposition of these theoretical explanations, with critical evaluations of their applicability to the problem of violence in modern society, are to be found in other publications, but it will be helpful to consider some of these concepts, taken from the results of research in the inter-related fields of psychology, biology, ethology and social anthropology.

In the animal world, aggression is necessary for survival. One species preys on another in order to obtain food. Similarly, at the human level, violence is used to kill other creatures in order to provide food and other substances believed to be necessary for survival.

A second function of aggression is the defence of offspring against predatory attack, thereby ensuring the preservation of the species. The equivalent in human behaviour is observed in the priority given to securing the safety of children in times of war.

In locations where adverse geographical or climatic conditions impose severe limitations on the available food supply, some species demonstrate a form of natural aggression which is directly related to survival needs. Sick, wounded or elderly members of the group are attacked and killed or left to die. The defective member would be a burden on the rest, consuming scarce food or retarding the group to its peril. It has to be eliminated for the safety of the rest.

This phenomenon occurs in those human societies which are endeavouring to survive in the harshest of conditions. Among certain Eskimo groups, the elderly were left to die on the ice when they were no longer able to contribute to the group's survival. Sick or wounded members of groups of survivors at sea have been put overboard in order to give the rest a better chance of rescue.

If this behaviour differs from the more usual interpretation of violence, the difference is only quantitative, since physical force is employed to commit an aggressive act which results in the death of a fellow member of the species.

In the natural world, violence is apparent in the competition for sexual partners. This usually takes the form of conflicts between the younger physically mature male members of the species to obtain the most desirable females. The probability that the latter are the more fertile and, therefore, the more likely to produce healthy offspring, is conducive to the survival of the species. These conflicts sometimes extend to struggles for supremacy and leadership, with the most powerful member asserting overall control. Among humans the competition for sexual partners sometimes results in violence. Does not the dance hall often provide the scene for a fight?

Recognised forms of achievement exist in most societies, such as the performance of deeds of physical prowess. In more complex societies, such as our own, such prowess might be demonstrated on the sports field. In both cases aggression takes a physical form, which is violence, even if performed within certain socially acceptable rules and with social approval and encouragement.

Where the expectations of society and the rules of the game of survival require types of apparently non-violent achievement, such as the passing of examinations or the acquisition of the skills of a trade, natural aggression has to be converted into appropriate motivation. Whatever the requirements of the social system, aggression is necessary in order to meet them.

Closely associated with these natural uses of violence for survival is violence to acquire and retain territory. Territoriality is one of the most interesting areas of animal and human behaviour. The animal must assert control over an area sufficiently large to provide the food and other resources, such as nest-building material or breeding-grounds, which are required. There is competition from other members of the same species as well as danger from predators. At breeding times, therefore, the animal has to use violence to drive away competitors and other invaders.

Many species of animal lay claim to territory and indicate its boundaries by such methods as urinating or defecating at certain points. These deposits act as chemical markers, visually apparent, or more often apparent by smell, to warn off the intending intruder. In a similar manner, teenage gangs in the large urban areas are aggressively and possessively conscious of their territories, often marking their claim to these with slogans of possession or defiance written on the walls.

The need to acquire territory is not confined, therefore, to the animal world. Nor is violence resulting from territoriality only a feature of large groups. It occurs very much at the level of the individual. Most of us, having found an empty railway compartment for our journey, tend to feel at least a little dismayed and even resentful if strangers join us at the next station. We know that we have no legal or moral right to the whole compartment, yet our feelings are disturbed by this invasion of our personal space. Similarly, we mark the limits of our territory by fences and walls, which give us feelings of security and privacy. The human story provides the best, or should it be the worst, examples of territoriality. Few, if any wars in history were fought with purposes other than the gaining or regaining of territory, or for the assertion of control over the people and resources of some part of our planet's surface. Gunpowder was once defined as a substance used in marking the boundary lines of nations!

Studies of animal populations have shown that intra-species violence increases with population density. The more animals there are in a given area, the higher the rate of violent conflict. This phenomenon, too, probably has a protective function, by reducing the size of the population to viable proportions in relation to the available resources. Research on prison populations and human groups in other institutional settings has demonstrated this, while there is a clear correlation between population density and communal violence in the cities. When the long-smouldering Northern Ireland troubles burst into flame in 1969, with the repression of the civil rights protest, the density of population within the limits of the city of Belfast was among the highest in Europe, owing to the inadequacies of slum clearance and re-housing policies.

Thus, while violence may be normal aggressive behaviour, helping to solve the major problems of survival, in the animal world, there are parallels at the human level. In violence between individuals and among groups and nations, the same themes recur. However, consideration must be given to the means by which violence may be inhibited or controlled in the human, and the learning processes by which this control is achieved.

In the physical and psychological characteristics of normal humanity, there is a very wide range of individual differences. The variability in the size and shape of people is sufficient to demonstrate this. These individual differences are also to be found in the less obvious characteristics of our bodily make-up, such as the brain, the nervous system and those complex physiological systems which underlie thought processes, learning and emotion.

The biological bases of emotion have been extensively explored, and the neurophysiological mechanisms have been largely identified, to explain differences in temperament and in the degree of emotion which the organism can experience. The fund of aggression available to be expressed varies from one individual to another, as does the readiness with which that aggression can be stimulated and released, and the ease with which it might be controlled by the restraints of conscience.

Conscience is a function of those parts of the brain and nervous system which are concerned with emotional behaviour. We feel our consciences, we do not think our consciences. Perceptual and conceptual processes might be involved and certain beliefs, with regard to appropriate behaviours, might result, but the actual experience of conscience is the emotion of fear or anxiety.

Feelings of anxiety in the earliest years of life are experienced in response to the absence of the loved parent figure, with whom a bond of affection has already been well established and on whom the child is dependent for security. Anxiety is similarly aroused when that flow of security-giving love from the parent is apparently cut off, which is how the child interprets the parent's anger or disapproval when he is naughty. This anxiety, moreover, is associated with the behaviour, on his part, which has caused this apparent withdrawal of love. Association of the naughty behaviour with the loss of love results, sooner or later, in a conditioned response effect, whereby the opportunity to commit that particular piece of naughtiness, or even the contemplation of it, is sufficient to elicit the feeling of anxiety.

What is conscience-arousing for one individual, however, will not necessarily have the same effect on another. This will depend on the selection of behaviours of which the parental figure has disapproved, or conversely, those behaviours of which the parent has approved and for which the child has been rewarded. As the child develops he comes into contact with other parent substitutes and authority figures from the adult world, such as school-teachers. If he has already internalised the values of his parents and has identified emotionally with them, as happens with most children fortunate enough to be brought up in a normal home and family, this effect generalises to those other impressive, benign authority figures. The conditioning process continues, and values and standards are acquired and internalised, to become part of his own feelings. Consequently, attitudes to others and the value system of his socio-cultural environment become part of his personality. If these standards include prohibitions on acts of violence, or on the outward expression of aggression, such actions will be inhibited by internalised conscience restraints. If, on the other hand, he has been brought up in a culture which approves of violent deeds and which encourages young people to act aggressively, or which, by its traditions and belief systems, reinforces hostility towards other groups, he will be motivated to commit acts of violence against them. In such circumstances, the perpetrator will be unrestrained by conscience and will be likely, moreover, to experience the enhancement of his self-esteem with his achievement.

A young man in the forests of New Guinea might be expected to bring back the head of a man from the next valley. By doing so, the young man will receive the approval of the tribe. Failure to commit this act of violence will meet with disapproval and in his case would be disturbing to his conscience. Some of the tit-for-tat sectarian murders in Northern Ireland have closely resembled this type of head-hunting behaviour, and apparently have had the approval of some members of the tribal sub-cultures from which the killers have come. The majority of the population of these islands find such acts of killing repugnant. Yet, in other circumstances, a considerable proportion of them might endorse killing on a much larger scale, in supporting military action against other nations in times of war. Conscience, therefore, acts selectively, depending on the standards of the culture, and cannot be regarded as representing any universal norm – even if the underlying neurophysiological mechanisms are the same throughout humanity.

It must be remembered, too, that while there is a wide range of variation in physical biological endowment, there is also wide variation in the types of family and social environment in which the earlier formative years are spent. Each receives training for life which differs to some degree from that of everybody else. These factors can account for the differences in propensity to violence and in the specific circumstances likely to contribute to the release of violent behaviour.

We have seen how aggression in the natural world is used in problem-solving, the problem being that of survival. Problems are sources of frustration until they are solved, and there is a

recognised    causal    relationship    between    frustration    and
aggression.

Most of the frustrations which we encounter in daily life are so
trivial that they do not trouble us, or else they are of such a nature
that the problem which they present can be easily solved. If our
road is blocked by a traffic accident, we take an alternative route.
If there is no suitable alternative, we are likely to generate more
aggression, for the frustration is greater. We are more likely to
complain to the traffic policeman, who is re-directing us, or to
express our aggression, at least verbally, towards the participants
in the accident for their stupidity and carelessness. We might also
react angrily to some irrelevant comment offered by our travelling companion. We might even blame ourselves for not setting
off sooner, which would have enabled us to pass the place before
the accident occurred. Our frustration tolerance threshold, the
capacity to experience frustration without generating aggressive
feeling, will have been exceeded.

Levels of frustration tolerance vary from one individual to
another. They vary depending on the nature of the frustration
and on other incidental factors, such as fatigue, hunger, thirst, or
other physical or emotional upset, stress or deprivation.

Illness or disability, in general, lowers frustration tolerance.
Some illnesses impose a range of frustrations, pain, physical
restriction and anxiety. In addition, the patient experiences
frustration in not being allowed to eat the food he likes, and in
having to take medicines which he does not like, as well as having
to submit to a variety of unpleasant, painful or embarrassing
ministrations at the hands of the medical and nursing professions.

Contrary to popular belief, violence is not a common feature of
the behaviour of patients suffering from the more severe mental
illnesses. Certainly, in the context of a psychotic episode, such as
an acute schizophrenic illness, the patient's perceptions and
beliefs are often irrationally distorted. He might hear voices
(auditory hallucinations) which tell him that someone intends to
harm him, in which case he might attack that person. He might
have grossly distorted beliefs regarding himself and his role and,
in attempting to act these out, might find himself in conflict with
others, in circumstances in which he might become violent. Some
very depressed patients develop delusions (false, unmodifiable,

preoccupying beliefs) which make them feel so evil and guilty that they believe that the evil affects other members of the family. Such patients have been known to take their own lives after taking the lives of their nearest and dearest. However, this type of violence, in the context of a severe mental illness, is comparatively rare.

In certain states of drug intoxication, similar distortions of perceptual processes and belief may result in disordered behaviour Here again, violence is secondary to the patient's attempts to act out his delusions. Some drugs, including alcohol, have the effect of releasing the personality from the controlling influence of their internalised restraints. Alcohol and other intoxicating substances may also have the effect of impairing capacity for judgment. The result may be that feelings of hostility, resulting from previous experiences of frustration, are released into physical action in the form of violence.

Certain illnesses and medical conditions are particularly noted for their association with a low frustration tolerance. Patients who have undergone a severe head injury with brain damage almost always show a marked increase in irritability, regardless of what other symptoms, disabilities and changes in personality are also being exhibited. Severely brain-damaged patients, particularly during the early stages of recovery, when the controlling areas of the brain are not yet functioning well enough, can behave with marked irrationality and violence, which they themselves are usually unable to recall at later stages of their recovery. Certain types of epilepsy are also associated with apparently unmotivated outbursts of violence.

Similarly, low frustration tolerance is often a feature of persons who have been brought up in institutional care and who, despite the substitute parenting which the caring services have endeavoured to provide, have not enjoyed the consistent parental encouragement and guidance which the child brought up in the more usual family setting has had the better fortune to receive.

Personalities distorted to whatever degree by organic brain conditions, and personalities crippled by inadequacies and abnormalities of their earlier upbringing, and whose behaviour, in consequence, shows this reduced frustration tolerance, do not necessarily commit acts of overt physical violence. Very often, there is a characteristic lack of persistence in facing the problems of life. This may be apparent in their limited efforts in the work situation, or in frequent altercations with work-mates or in disputes with managers and other authority figures. It may reveal itself, too, in other situations where the skills of interpersonal behaviour are required to solve normal day to day problems, as in some cases of marital breakdown, with the inability of one personality to adjust to the needs and characteristics of the other.

Where, as a result of illness, injury or personality defects, there is overt violent aggression (and this occurs in only a small proportion of cases), the aggression can take an intropunitive form, with self-injury and even self-destruction, physical aggression towards others being less frequent. Even where the aggression takes the form of extrapunitive violence, it may well be violence against property and not against persons.

In the example of the road accident, our aggression was directed not only at the source of the frustration, the incompetent motorist, but also towards the policeman and towards our companion. Neither of these had frustrated us, but they were available and we directed our aggression against them. Directing aggression towards a substitute target, or scapegoat, is a common behavioural mechanism, occurring where the original source of the frustration is not available, or where it would be imprudent to attack it.

There are numerous ways in which scapegoats are used to receive the aggression generated by day-to-day frustrations. Opponents are used as scapegoats in the course of playing games. In some sports, both opponent and the ball provide this service. Aggression is vented on them with varying degrees of violence, so that disturbing aggressive feelings are expressed in a non-harmful way. As the spectator identifies with a player or team, his aggression is expressed vicariously on to the members of the opposing team. The spectator who shouts abusively at the players or at the referee is ridding himself of aggressive feelings which might have been accumulating within him from a variety of other sources of frustration. The players and the referee come to no harm (usually), while the spectator's interpersonal relationships in the rest of his life are still safe, and he feels better by being rid of the aggressive feelings. The scapegoat mechanism provides a safety valve for the harmless expression of aggression in society. This same process operates when we identify with characters in films, plays and stories. The satisfaction which the viewer experiences when the hero of the western film beats the villain to the draw, in the ritual gunfight, or knocks him down in the bar-room brawl, might be, in part, the satisfaction of expressing his own need for aggression through identification with the hero and on to the scapegoat villain. Here again the effect, in terms of the viewer's emotional health, is beneficial, since he is rid of his aggression, while nobody in reality has suffered.

In the road accident example, part of our reaction was to blame ourselves. Self-directed or intropunitive aggression is a common tendency, depending partly on previous learning experiences and partly on the immediate circumstances.

Some psychiatric patients, such as those suffering from depressive illnesses, will express considerable self-criticism. Sometimes there may be a limited degree of validity in their self-blame but, in their depressively disturbed emotional state, this is the only aspect of themselves which they are able to see. Others offer grossly exaggerated versions of their own faults and suffer excessive guilt, sometimes over trivial misdeeds, sometimes over sins which are wholly imaginary. Others, partly as a consequence of this depressive intropunitive misperception of themselves, will commit acts which are punishment-seeking, such as shop-lifting of trivial articles in which they have no other interest than as an unconscious means of obtaining blame and punishment. It is in the context of deep depression that patients act out the ultimate in self-destructive violence – suicide.

Patients suffering psychosomatic illnesses experience con-ditions which, as the term suggests, have both mental and bodily components. Among the more obvious examples are certain types of dermatitis, some asthmas, some forms of ulcer and some other gastro-intestinal conditions. The physical disorder in each case is real, but there is also a contributory factor in the personality of the patient. Psychosomatic patients tend to be intropunitive in their characteristic responses to stress and frustration. They often carry considerable responsibility very conscientiously, but allow themselves little outlet for their feelings of aggression. This acts internally to cause physical damage to body tissues, or to interfere with life-preserving processes. The psychosomatic patient is behaving, perhaps unconsciously, with violence towards himself.

Elements of intropunitive violence have been seen, by some, in the effects of race riots and other communal strife, particularly where damage to property has occurred, apparently caused by members of the ethnic minority groups themselves. Whether it is valid to claim that destruction of property within one's own territory is a form of intropunitive aggression is debatable. Usually the damage has been associated with looting by those whose interest in the events has been more criminal than political, or else the damage has been for barricading defensive purposes against real or imaginary attack, as in some of the riots in Northern Ireland. Often, too, the damage has been to buildings which have a symbolic function, being perceived by the rioters as representative of the order of authority responsible for their frustrations.

A considerable amount of self-directed violence is to be found among prison inmates. The frustrations which prisoners experience take many forms. Although the reaction is often expressed in extrapunitive hostility, with violence towards staff or other prisoners, or towards the furnishings, there is also a high rate of deliberate self-injury. This ranges from scratching of the wrists to major deliberate self-injury by cutting, scalding, burning, limb fracturing, and so on. A constant risk within any prison is attempted suicide, and actual suicides are not infrequent. Self-directed violence is even commoner among female prisoners than it is among the male prison population.

When considering violence among prisoners, it must be remembered that convicted offenders are not a homogeneous population in terms of age, socio-cultural background, intelligence, educational attainments, personality, or the type of crime for which they have been convicted. They are, however, on the whole, a young adult population. Second, the majority of convicted offenders come from less privileged social backgrounds. Third, the average intelligence of the offender population is significantly lower than the average for the general population, and, moreover, their average level of educational attainment is lower than their own intelligence average. In other words, while most convicted offenders are of below average intelligence, they are also educationally backward, even by comparison with their own intellectual capacity. A considerable number are almost totally illiterate.

The research evidence on the personality of offenders is by no means conclusive. However, there is evidence of above average tendencies for impulsivity, comparatively poor capacity for internalisation of values, and a more marked variability in the generation of emotion. While these would be generalisations from studies of populations of convicted offenders, we must exclude those who are labelled terrorist, or whose convictions have been for political reasons. Terrorists and political prisoners, of whatever persuasion or cause, do not necessarily resemble the offender population on these measures.

A further distinction should be made between those imprisoned for holding or promulgating beliefs which conflict with those in political power, and terrorists imprisoned for taking violent action for an alleged political cause. Political prisoners throughout the world tend to be more intelligent and better educated than the general population of convicted criminals.

Persons convicted of terrorist offences in Northern Ireland would tend to resemble the non-political offenders described above. In general, they come from the same impoverished sociocultural environments characterised by chronic mass unemployment. They are usually of below average intelligence and of limited educational attainment. Boredom and lack of opportunity in their lives, together with their limited horizons and lack of social sophistication, all contribute to a readiness to participate in ill-considered escapades, sometimes at the suggestion of more sinister figures, but often as impulsive, temporarily exciting acts of bravado.

It is comparatively easy for the security forces to apprehend these less competent terrorists and comparatively easy, moreover, to obtain confessions from them sufficient to convict them for their offence, and sometimes for other offences too. Violence has probably occurred at some stage in the offence, and further violence might have been experienced by the terrorist offender in the process of apprehension, interrogation and conviction. Consequently, the further frustration to which he has been subjected will have generated more aggression. If, moreover, he believes that he has been unjustly convicted and that the authorities have no moral or legal basis, his resentment and contempt for the regime and its servants are increased. In many cases, individual members of the security forces, who have been injured or assassinated, have been the consequential scapegoats.

The disturbed socio-political situation which contributes to terrorist violence also provides opportunities for the acting out of private conflicts and personal vendettas, under the guise of political cause. Moreover, it is not uncommon for psychiatrically disturbed or psychopathic personalities, with personal needs for violence, to gravitate to the paramilitary gang where they may achieve brief fame and notoriety before their own actions are terminated by further violence.

Those with sadistic needs to inflict pain and cause fear can find their outlets in the protection rackets and intimidation to which the people of the poorer areas are subjected. Here, too, violence against persons or property to effect compliance with political strategy, or to fund paramilitary action, can sometimes be the cloak for the satisfaction of individual emotional needs, as well as an opportunity for personal acquisitive crime.

The majority of non-political convicted offenders have committed crimes of acquisition, such as larceny, with violence associated with their primary offence only in a small proportion of cases. This violence has often been secondary to the failure of the crime, or has become necessary owing to the resistance of the victim, or some other incidental factor, as for example with the potential burglar, who is discovered on the premises by the owner, and who then commits violence in order to escape. Premeditated or planned violence occurs only infrequently compared with the great number of solved and unsolved crimes of acquisition of property, which take place every year. Moreover, the convict population, including those convicted for terrorist offences, is a biased population of unsuccessful offenders – unsuccessful in that they have been detected, apprehended and convicted. Successful offenders, whether violent or not, and whether political or not, are not in prison!

Where the parties to a dispute do not have the intellectual and verbal capacity for argument, and the problem cannot be solved at the level of verbal interaction, there is the greater likelihood of resort to more primitive behaviour, with the use of physical force. Those from more disadvantaged backgrounds, with below average intelligence and limited educational attainment, are employed, if they are employed at all, in manual, unskilled work. They earn their living and solve the problem of survival by the use of their hands and their muscle power. If faced with the frustration of someone who disagrees with them, they are likely to make a characteristically physical response. Thus we find that violence to settle disagreements occurs much more often with those who are less verbally articulate, where communication by other than physical means is not available. There is, for example, a very high rate of interpersonal violence among those who are deaf and dumb.

The importance of language in relation to the use of violence cannot be over-emphasised. The more a person is able to explain himself, the more confident and the less frustrated he feels. The wider his vocabulary, the easier it is for him to express subtle shades of meaning and feeling. He can convey needs, wishes, fears, likes and dislikes, without the risk of misunderstanding and conflict. The violence that occurs within families and within marriages is often the consequence, at least in part, of the inability of the parties to express themselves accurately and meaningfully. Where the frustration at the level of verbal communication becomes total, the more primitive response of movement is more likely, with separation from the frustration by walking out. In some cases the movement takes the form of violence. The frustration–aggression–scapegoat sequence is clearly apparent in much of what is recognised today as intra-family violence and in the more recently recognised battered wives and battered babies syndromes.

The nervous system increases the organism's capacity for physical activity in anxiety-provoking situations. In man's evolutionary pre-history, this had a usefulness, since most anxiety-provoking situations would then have been situations of physical danger. This process still operates, although the anxiety-provoking situation may not be one where the capacity to run more quickly or to fight more forcefully is likely to be helpful. The person who anxiously awaits news will have a raised activity level, experienced subjectively as a need for action and exhibited in a higher rate of pacing, smoking or talking. It can be transformed into aggressive behaviour, as is sometimes shown by clients towards the staff of Social Security offices and Employment Centres. Often, this violence is quite atypical of the client's more usual behaviour. He is anxious, he is limited in his understanding of the procedures, owing to his poor verbal ability, together with the impairment of his capacity to take in information (another effect of anxiety). He cannot understand what the officer is trying to tell him. He is aware, moreover, of feelings of social and educational inferiority and that he is less successful and in general less advantaged than the officer. He has had to undergo humiliation, waiting in a queue with other 'social failures', and he is likely to feel that the officer looks down on him, or suspects him of deception or laziness. When he is told, probably quite correctly, that he does not qualify or that his form is incorrectly completed, he responds to this frustration with aggressive violence, aided by the urge for activity provided by his aroused nervous system.

In an age of higher levels of unemployment, society still emphasises success and achievement. To be a non-achiever is, therefore, an extremely frustrating experience. For some, this comes as the result of enforced redundancy, often with partial destruction of a way of life. Self-esteem is further undermined by the implied loss of value in the eyes of others. Loss of self-esteem, together with the loss of economic status as a wage-earner, alters the concept of self in a depressive, intropunitive direction, increasing the vulnerability to psychosomatic and depressive illness.

For others, particularly the younger unemployed, the lack of opportunity for the achievement and self-assertion necessary for an adequate self-concept presents frustration, to which the response might take an outwardly aggressive form. Furthermore, there is not only the fund of youthful emotion, but also a fund of physical energy, seeking an outlet. As noted already, violence occurs with greater frequency in the young, the less well-educated, the less well-off and the less adequate. Feelings of inferiority stimulate a need for compensation in alternative achievement. The emphasis on achievement, as measured by wealth and material goods, is apparent, not only in our educational and occupational systems, but also in those even more potent influences, the communication media, particularly television.

For previous generations, information and entertainment were obtained by hearing, the auditory modality, or via the eyes, provided that one could read. With the advent of television, however, an information medium was introduced into the home for which no reading ability was necessary, and which presented its message via the visual modality as well as the auditory. This was a much more powerful influence on beliefs, standards, values and aspirations, an influence augmented more recently by the video.

While all sections of society have been affected, it is the less well-educated, the less socially adequate, the unemployed and comparatively unsophisticated young person who is most likely to be impressed. Moreover, the message which these media convey, whether via political propaganda or in the values demonstrated in the transatlantic soap opera, emphasises the importance of the acquisition and display of wealth, while advertisements claim to know what successful people today should possess in order to demonstrate their achievements and adequacy.

The unemployed, the socially unfortunate, the emotionally unstable, the under-privileged, the members of the ethnic minorities, whose advancement is blocked, all know that if they remain well-behaved, conforming citizens in today's world, they have no hope of ever achieving what television tells them they must have in order to be worthy. Prestige and esteem are to be acquired by money and possessions, but there are no legitimate avenues to these for the under-achievers and the under-privileged. This frustration is perfectly suited to generate aggression. To this must be added the fund of energy available and the boredom and lack of challenge in their life circumstances.

Injustice, inequality, discontent, protest and violence have always featured in our country's history. For former generations, however, emigration or enlistment with the colours or the fleet were safety valves which enabled many of the younger and more energetic malcontents to act out their aggression overseas. The nation's enemies, or the indigenous populations of the former colonial empire, were their scapegoats. This outlet is no longer available, although it could be claimed that the unnecessary violence on the part of some of our soldiers in Northern Ireland is a remnant of these practices.

Moreover, the major improvements in health and nutrition since the second world war have resulted in a healthier, more energetic, young population than in former times, a population whose physical maturation into young adulthood is taking place earlier, and a population with more unfilled time and a heightened awareness of what it lacks, in a society which sets unattainable goals. Achievement and self-assertion have, therefore, to be sought in other ways, in risk-taking behaviours and more primitive tribal ritual battles.

Much of what is called 'football hooliganism' derives from this. Tribalism is evident in the use of colours and emblems, together with taunting partisan chants, often intended to offend supporters of the opposing team and even to provoke them to violent reaction. The frustration–aggression sequence is clearly evident in much of the destructive vandalism which has been associated with these phenomena. Violence by football fans, whether against persons or property, has usually been far more extensive when their team has lost. Second, the violence and vandalism usually occurs when the team is playing away from home, when the supporters are in the territory of their opponents. Creatures, whether human or animal, are more physiologically alerted when out of their own territory. Anxiety levels for some are higher, and anxiety can elicit aggression.

To be in enemy territory can be anxiety-provoking, but can also provide an opportunity for risk-taking by taunting the opposition or the police, or by deeds of daring which would win acclaim and help to compensate for feelings of inadequacy and unimportance. For the young unemployed in contemporary British society, and for those in boring jobs, with little, if any, prospects of significant self-advancement, participation in these tribal rituals and the risk-taking, particularly if violence ensues, offers one of the few opportunities for achievement and excitement.

In the Northern Ireland situation, tribalism and territoriality are clearly associated with the violence. Although superficially it may appear to derive from religious differences, it is essentially a tribal conflict, with religious affiliation acting as the membership badge by which the two sides are to be distinguished from each other. Territories are clearly recognisable from the tribal markings on the walls, ranging from the most simple daubings and letters – 'IRA', 'UVF' – and phrases sometimes mis-spelt – 'Brits Out', 'No Pope Here', 'Pasiley is our Leader' – to much more sophisticated and often artistically complex murals. These might depict the plight of Republican prisoners with associated slogans of defiance in the Nationalist green districts, while highly ornate paintings of William of Orange adorn the gable ends in Unionist Orange districts.

The quantity of slogan-daubing and wall-painting increases the further down the social class scale, but so, too, does the quantity of violence. The better-off middle-class areas have less of these visual cues of tribal identity, but here the two affiliations interact more easily and, on the whole, have levels of education and social sophistication which render unnecessary the more overtly violent type of display. The middle-class population is cushioned by its comparative socio-economic advantage from the frustrating stresses of unemployment, to which the inhabitants of the poorer areas are subject, and which fuel much of their aggression. They are, moreover, less susceptible to the firebrand propaganda and simplistic solutions of the tribal political agitators.

Territorial slogan graffiti, with their implicit threat of violence, are to be observed not only in Northern Ireland, but wherever the under-privileged feel it necessary to protest. For some, they may act as another safety valve mechanism, substituting violent words or threats in the place of real physical violence. The literature of the world, after all, is replete with the expression of violent feelings, satire, lampoon and diatribe. Man's superior brain can be utilised for aggressive expression, obviating the need for physical violence which would have been more species-destructive. Whether the writing of threats to outsiders or claims to territorial possession can fulfil this function, is questionable. Slogans and other visual symbols of territorial claims, such as flags, can themselves be provocative causes of violence.

For many years, involvement in tribal hostility in Northern Ireland has provided an outlet for aggression for the less sophisticated social groups, whether of orange or green identity. This has usually taken the form of non-violent aggression in tribal ceremonial marches, with neo-militaristic trappings and partisan songs by religio-political organisations such as the Orange Order and the Ancient Order of Hibernians. The overt activities of these sometimes have a territorial function in asserting dominance within areas of the country where that tribe has a numerical majority. Sometimes, the march will extend to areas with a sufficient number of the opposing tribe to risk a hostile reaction. This, in turn, provides the opportunity for physical violence for those who feel the need to asert themselves more vigorously or to indulge in risk-taking.

This violent assertion is not only more convincing and emotionally satisfying for the less intelligent, but also serves a purpose of providing evidence, where their members may need to be convinced, that there is indeed an external enemy whom they must unite to resist. Whether the outcome is violent or not, the need for assertion by a demonstration of unity and power is temporarily satisfied, compensating for feelings of inferiority and unimportance.

At other times in history and in other places, similar behaviours have been observed. A considerable proportion of the numerical strength of the growing Nazi party in the Germany of the 1930s was provided from the less well-off socio-economic groups, who resented their perceived insignificance. These responded to their frustrations by gravitating to a political movement which emphasised the assertion of power by physical violence when expedient, and by aggression against scapegoat targets, such as the Jews, and other social groups labelled as inferior. This aggression was to extend later to other nations. The concept of territoriality could have no clearer expression than Hitler's demand for 'Lebensraum'.

The territoriality and tribalism to be observed in Northern Ireland, particularly in the poorer urban back streets, can have a unifying and reassuring function. The emphasis on unity in the face of threat reinforces group cohesion and feelings of belongingness. This was clearly evident after 1969 in the tribal areas of Belfast and Derry, areas of generations of unemployment and socio-economic depression with both real and imaginary deprivations and under-privilege.

When the violence began, in response to the unnecessarily vigorous frustration of what were, initially, peaceful demonstrations for reform, counter-violence was released from the opposing tribal areas, with the acquiescence, if not the encouragement, of those in authority. Participation in group defensive activity was stimulated to such an extent that even the socially isolated and the psychiatrically depressed became involved. There was no measurable increase in the rate of admissions to psychiatric hospitals or in the rate of suicide. There is even a suggestion that the intropunitive aggression of the potentially suicidal depressive may have been diverted to an external target, and that the newly acquired feelings of belongingness were in some instances able to overcome the schizoid isolation of the socially-withdrawn patient, to allow him to participate again in his socio-cultural setting.

Unfortunately, any beneficial side-effects of the earlier violence were not to last. While hospital admission rates for the major psychiatric illnesses have remained consistent with general European norms, the effect of living in a situation of chronic violence in the dilapidated paramilitary-dominated urban areas is reflected in the rates of medical prescriptions of tranquillisers, anti-depressants and sedatives. Concern for the safety of other members of the family, particularly the anxiety of parents of teenagers, who are at risk of involvement with the paramilitaries, is particularly stressful and often more emotionally damaging than personal presence at a violent incident. Members of the security and prison services are at risk, not only from paramilitary attack, but, increasingly, from the development of acute depressive reactions. In an alarming number of cases, the weapons which they carry for protection have become the means of suicide.

In areas such as West Belfast, which have undergone mob invasion, army intervention, the unnecessary brutality of internment, mass arrests and destructive army searches (which incidentally provided potent recruitment propaganda for the paramilitaries), a legacy of social problems and social pathology remains. Nevertheless, even in these traumatised areas, individual differences in vulnerability have been clearly demonstrated, together with a remarkable resilience to trauma and stress. Those who have undergone personal violence, either at the hands of the paramilitaries or of the security forces following an arrest, and those who underwent the sensory deprivation interrogation procedures, similarly demonstrate a wide range of individual differences in the degree of response. Some have emerged apparently emotionally unscathed, while, at the other extreme, there are those with chronic and crippling anxiety neuroses. Among children, the effects have been equally varied. Children from the more disturbed districts have the highest school refusal rates and the highest rates of serious delinquency, but for others from those same areas, academic performance rates have been improving. This is attributed to a determination to obtain qualifications which will facilitate escape from this type of society, and to the control exerted by the more conscientious parents in keeping their children off the streets at times of unrest. Consequently, they spend more time at their homework!

Where inter-group hostility exists, the symbols of the opposing group can in themselves become stimuli for aggressive responses, as in the case of the football fans. At the simplest level, these aggression-eliciting stimuli might be flags, as in the Northern Ireland situation, but the extensive human learning capacity extends the process to include other symbolic representatives of the target. Consequently, political demonstrators or pickets in an industrial dispute might learn to make a discrimination between the police, as visually presented in the form of the benign bobby on the beat, and the police as visually presented en masse, visored, mounted and menacing in riot gear. The former appears as a reassuring safety-providing father-figure, whereas experiences of the latter have resulted in their being seen as the armed force of an unsympathetic, hostile and sometimes even alien authority.

Here, the police are seen not only as the symbolic representative of resented authority, but also as the available scapegoats. The missile-throwing rioter is expressing aggression for the way in which members of the police have previously treated him, by attacking other members of that same body. These processes have operated in incidents in Northern Ireland and in the disturbances involving members of ethnic minority groups and the police in Britain.

If the establishment of a strong bond of affection between parent and child provides a foundation for the learning of morality, obedience and consideration for the interests of others, then where that bond is never established, or where the parent has ceased to be held in affection, the conditioning is much weaker and less effective. Similarly, when institutions of authority lose the respect of those they govern, they and their symbolic representatives can become the targets of resentment, manifested in violent protest. Much of the violence which is expressed towards the police and security forces, whether in Britain, Northern Ireland, or elsewhere, derives from this loss of respect, as the population has become increasingly aware of deficiencies and hypocrisies of those in high places. When those in authority have to maintain their order by force and fear, they resemble the inadequate parent who has failed to achieve the love and respect of the child. When the institutions and customs of society divide rather than unite, differences are emphasised. Resentment, frustration and aggression are reinforced, and tribalism and sectional self-interest determine actions and attitudes.

The uniforms and face-concealing helmets of the riot police, or the uniforms and blackened faces of the soldiers in Northern Ireland, serve to reduce their individuality, and thereby to reduce their humanity in the perceptions of the potential attacker. The less a victim of aggression is identifiable as an individual human being like oneself, the more easily is aggression released. The more the victim is different, or appears to be different from the attacker, the less is the latter under the control of inhibiting mechanisms in his own personality.

In nature, those members of the same species which acquire a perceptible difference, resulting from injury or infirmity, are eliminated by the other members. In human societies, too, under extremities of stress, similar defensive destructive mechanisms operate to eliminate the defective.

The more the victim appears to be unlike the aggressor, the greater the perceived social distance betweeen them, and the weaker the restraints on the aggression. In the training of combat troops, the enemy must be made to appear different, in order to overcome whatever qualms of conscience the trainee infantryman might have about killing a fellow human being. 'Hate the stranger' feelings, deriving from our evolutionary pre-history, have to be re-awakened, just as the Nazis emphasised the alleged inferiority and the defects of their captive populations in order to motivate the staff of their extermination camps.

The same mechanisms operate when we feel resentment, distrust or suspicion of those human beings who are obviously different from us in their presentation, whether they be physically handicapped, mentally handicapped, have a different coloured skin a different regional accent, dress differently, or hold different religious or political views.

Man's technological advance has produced more efficient tools with which to kill on a grander scale, without the opportunity for any restraining face-to-face contact. The more remote and invisible the victim is, the easier it is for the aggressor to inflict violence without feeling conscience-stricken. The man who drops the bomb in the high flying aircraft feels no distress at bombing the population below, for they are too far away to be perceived as human beings like himself.

The extent to which man has applied his superior intellect to the invention of complex technology, with which to achieve dominance over this planet, is one measure of his evolutionary development. Unfortunately, that technology has also provided the means of self-destruction without any commensurate application of intellect to the development of the techniques of living in civilised harmony. Violence, all too often, is the problem-solving technique of a humanity still limited to behaviours appropriate to a more primitive stage of evolutionary history. The Behavioural Sciences have made some progress in enabling us to understand the causes of violence, and have even begun to examine how violence may be controlled. Nevertheless, we still live on a planet where as much of its wealth is spent in a year on health welfare and education as is spent every two hours on armaments and the technologies of death and destruction. Belloc's 'Ultima Ratio' is not yet obsolete.

## REFERENCES

Berkowitz, L. (Ed.), *Roots of Aggression*, New York, Atherton Press, 1969.

Blackburn, R. 'Mentally Disordered Offenders' in Liddell A. (ed.), *The Practice of Clinical Psychology in Great Britain*, John Wiley & Sons Ltd., 1983.

Eysenck, H.J. 'Current Theories of Crime' in Karas E. (ed.), *Current Issues in Clinical Psychology*, Vol. I, New York, Plenum, 1983.

Feldman, M.P. (Ed.), *Criminal Behaviour*, Vol. I, Chichester, Wiley, 1982.

Feldman, M.P. (Ed.) *Developments in the Study of Criminal Behaviour*, Vol. 2: *Violence*, Chichester, Wiley, 1982.

Fraser, R.M., 'The Cost of Commotion: An Analysis of the Psychiatric Sequelae of the Belfast Riots', in *British Journal of Psychiatry*, March, 1971.

Gudjonsson, G.H. and Drinkwater, J., 'Intervention Techniques for Violent Behaviour', in Hollin, C. and Howells, K. (eds.), *Criminological and Legal Psychiatry*, No.9 issue.

Gunn, J., Robertson, G., and Way, C., *Psychiatric Aspects of Imprisonment*, London, Academic Press, 1978.

Harbison, J., (Ed.) *Children of the Troubles*, Belfast, Stranmillis Learning Resources Unit, 1984.

Harbison, J. and Harbison, J. (Eds.) *Society under Stress*, Wells, Somerset, Open Books, 1986.

Lorenz, K., *On Aggression*, London, Methuen & Co. Ltd., 1966.

Lyons, H.A., 'Psychiatric Sequelae of the Belfast Riots', in *British Journal of Psychiatry*, March, 1971.

Owens, R.G., and Ashcroft, J.B., *Violence. A Guide for the Caring Professions*, London, Croom Helm, 1985.

Storr, A., *Human Aggression*, Harmondsworth, Penguin Books, 1968.

# CHAPTER FIVE

# VIOLENCE AND PUBLIC DISORDER

## Richard Clutterbuck

### INTRODUCTION

You will have read elsewhere in this volume[1] that violence is certainly not a new phenomenon in our society. Acts of force or violence were by no means at odds with the way our forefathers lived their lives nor, for better or for worse, are they at variance with the way we collectively conduct ourselves today. This situation is reflected in the law. There are several examples where the law actually permits the use of force. The Criminal Law Act 1967, section 3, allows any person to use reasonable force in the prevention of crime or to effect a lawful arrest. It is this provision, for example, which allows use by the police of firearms. Home Office guidelines, published from time to time, currently indicate that firearms should be used only where there is good reason to suppose that a police officer may have to face a person who is armed or otherwise so dangerous that he could not safely be restrained without the use of firearms. Wherever practicable they are to be used after an oral warning and then only as a last resort. Thus although the use of deadly force is permitted it is also to be watched closely. Another example where the law permits the use of force is to be found in the Police and Criminal Evidence Act 1984, section 117, which permits a constable to use reasonable force, if necessary, in the exercise of such of his powers under that statute as do not require the consent of another. Perhaps it may be noted that the 1967 Act has no requirement that reasonable force be 'necessary', the 1984 Act includes that limitation. This may be taken as an indication that today we are looking more closely at violence or force, in whatever mode it arises.

There are occasions where the law may not actually authorise the use of force or violence, but nevertheless such conduct does not offend against the criminal code. The example of professional boxing comes readily to mind. Put simply, the object of the exercise is that two adults at the centre of a public meeting each intend to inflict actual, if not grievous, bodily harm on one another. At present it is tolerated within our society although it may today fall into the margins of moral acceptability. Times are changing and at some point in the future it may fall outside the moral and criminal codes. It is not even true today that any act of violence will fall merely within marginal acceptability. The law does not set its face against, nor does our current moral code reject, the infliction of corporal punishment within the bounds of reason by a parent on a child.

Thus it will be seen that our society cannot be said to be one which totally rejects violence or the use of force. The great problem for the law is to define what force is lawful or at least not contrary to law and what violence constitutes a criminal offence. The whole is complicated by the fact that though both the law and our society actually condone violence they do so only in certain circumstances. The violence or force may be the same in any number of circumstances, but the legality of its use may differ. The provisions of the Criminal Law Act 1967, section 3, actually permit the use of force. These are taken even to authorise the use of reasonable force against a police officer or a private citizen who is purporting to make an unlawful arrest. However the fact that there is such 'a right' to use force does not necessarily mean that the use of force is 'right'. This is clear from the statutory provision that the force should be reasonable. It must neither be used where the circumstances do not warrant force, nor must any force used be excessive in all the circumstances. Only if these conditions are fulfilled will it be 'right' to resort to 'a right' to use force in the eyes of the law.

In the eyes of society as a whole, whether it is 'right' to use force is a complex social question which cannot simply be determined by a barren consideration of the appropriate laws and legal rights. It is by no means uncommon today for those who feel that they are treated unfairly or wrongly to jump straight to 'a right' to use force or violence to redress their situation, even to the extent that they seek to generate such a right from the fact of the situation in which they find themselves. This is to entirely bypass the all-important question of whether it is 'right' to resort to violence or force. A careful consideration of all legal provisions, both statutory and common law, necessitates a positive answer to the question of whether it is right to use force before that force which the law permits in the abstract can be used with impunity.

In general the law does not condone the use of force or violence. This is subject to exceptions. These exceptions are narrow, and either explicit or implicit in them is the requirement that it is 'right' to use force. The law sets its face against violence or force except in defined situations. It would be a misconception to look at these exceptions and from them build a picture of a society which is generally tolerant of violence; the opposite is true, and the evolutionary trend of our society tends to reinforce this interpretation. As society moves towards a more ordered state so this will be reflected in both the laws adopted and the law as put into practice. The more complex our society becomes the greater will be the disruption to ordered living which violence causes.

The paper that follows is broadly divided into a consideration of issues of context and an appraisal of the laws themselves. In the former category I have outlined the dualism which exists in our attitude today to violence, a dualism which is most marked when we consider distinctions between legitimate and illegitimate violence or force. In addition, no study of legal aspects of violence should be contemplated without a consideration of the practical parameters within which the law must operate, and this is included towards the end. The central sections of the paper deal with the laws themselves, both the substantive laws and the laws of prevention. They cannot be understood without realising the vital importance of the factor of discretion. The law is not static, and a section is included to cover the current proposals for reform enshrined in the Public Order Bill.

VIOLENCE IN CONTEXT

In his report on the Red Lion Square Disorders in June 1974,[2]

Lord Scarman includes in his list of first principles a fundamental human right to public order and tranquillity: see paras 5 and 6. This is a necessary concomitant of civilised living. However it would be an error to focus solely on the words which Lord Scarman uses, namely 'order' and 'tranquillity', for he goes on to describe a balance which must be sought, in his particular case between protest and public order. It is that balance which is at the heart of his notion of civilised living. In other words civilised living is both the product of order and tranquillity and also determines what is meant by the words order and tranquillity. Civilised living can only take place in a more or less ordered society and the degree of order required is that which allows the ordinary citizen to go about his business and pleasure without obstruction or inconvenience. There is thus no right to 'tranquillity' in absolute form nor to 'order', without more.

In terms of disorder this can readily be demonstrated. For example, consider a citizen who rushes from his home into the street and jumps up and down shouting at the top of his voice, 'I've won a million on the pools!'. He is causing disruption, noise and palpable disorder, yet he probably commits no offence. Indeed one authority[3] offers the opinion that there is no substantive offence known to English common law of simply breaking the peace without more. Thus conduct which by any definition is 'disorderly' is in fact brought within our notions of living within an ordered society.

At first sight it may appear that any violent act or any act involving physical force by one citizen on another, perpetrated in the public domain, would run counter to the right which we enjoy to live our lives in an ordered and tranquil society. Prima facie the law would seem to accept this. The tort, or civil wrong, of battery may be committed merely by touching another who does not consent. The criminal law defines the offence of battery in similar terms, namely the infliction of personal violence by one citizen on another where violence includes minimal contact.[4]

However we all accept as part of our daily lives the inevitable jostling and use of physical force inherent, for example, in a trip on the London underground. Such falls within our notion of an ordered society. No one would reasonably contemplate a civil action for damages in such circumstances. The same is recognised

by the criminal law. In *Donelly* v *Jackman* (1970)[5] a police officer
tapped a member of the public, D, on the shoulder in order to
draw the latter's attention to the fact that the officer wanted to
speak with him. D then struck the officer with some force and
was convicted of assaulting a police officer in the execution of
his duty. He appealed unsuccessfully to the Queen's Bench
Divisional Court on the basis that the police officer was not acting
in the course of his duty in tapping him on the shoulder. Mr.
Justice Talbot expressed the view that 'it is not every trivial
interference with a citizen's liberty which amounts to a course of
conduct sufficient to take the officer out of the course of his duty'.
These 'trivial' acts of force are part of our daily lives and are
generally accepted as such, so that no one can complain about
them in themselves.

In certain contexts we accept something more than 'trivial
interferences', for example in sport. After a particularly vigorous
encounter at Twickenham in 1980 between the rugby union
teams representing England and Wales, the Chief Constable
of Greater Manchester, Mr. James Anderton, in a letter to
*The Times*[6] commented unfavourably on the many violent acts
perpetrated by the players on the field of play, witnessed
by a large crowd and several million television viewers. Mr.
Anderton seemed to express the view that if such conduct had not
taken place in the context of an England versus Wales rugby
International then serious criminal charges would have been
warranted. The underlying premise on which Mr. Anderton's
comments are based is that violence in the context of a currently
acceptable sport can be brought within notions of an ordered
society. To this extent violent conduct between citizens can be
and is tolerated both by the law and by ourselves as individuals.
Yet his letter is also evidence that current notions of acceptability
are neither static nor beyond criticism.

If we take the matter a little further, Mr. Anderton apparently
characterised what took place as 'a game of rugby' and thus, for
better or worse, to be tolerated as such. This is not however to
state that any act which takes place in the context of a rugby game
is to be taken to fall within the four corners of acceptable and
lawful conduct. If a player uses excessive force or causes serious
injury to an opponent in an unconscionable way, for example by a

deliberate kick in the face which causes blindness, then it is very likely, notwithstanding what Mr. Anderton said, that serious criminal charges would be brought in the circumstances even of a game of rugby, as indeed they have been – see for example *R* v *Billinghurst* (1970),[7] where a rugby player was successfully prosecuted for causing grievous bodily harm during a game.

In this latter situation the law focuses on the violence and not on the rugby. If what is done is characterised as criminal force or violence or, for that matter, as disorder, then the criminal law is brought into play. The fact that the violence took place in the context of a rugby match is irrelevant. This is true in other situations. If for example damage is done to property it is no concern of the law insofar as criminality is concerned whether the damage is caused by a football hooligan or by a deeply sincere political protester. If violent disorder breaks out in the streets the law determines criminality not according to the motives of those acting in that way, be they greatly deprived, politically sincere or simply out of control, the law focuses simply on the fact of disorder. Motives may on occasions however be relevant at the sentencing stage. In short the law denies all knowledge of species of violence or disorder, once conduct is characterised as violence or disorder the law focuses on this alone. It is frequently the case that those of the most sincere views feel that the 'justice' of their cause or plight legitimates their conduct, but as pointed out above there are many steps between the notions, 'I am right' and 'I have the right to use force' and 'it is right to do so'.

## THE FACTOR OF DISCRETION

If we return to Mr. Anderton's letter, he may have been critical of the conduct of the players, he does not appear to have been critical of any decision by those police officers present not to invoke the criminal law. This is rightly so. The law on public order is entirely bound up with the exercise of discretion by those whose duty it is to enforce the law; that is the police, the prosecutors and the courts. With regard to the criminal law generally the notion that there could ever be complete enforcement has long been discredited. With regard to the laws relating to public order there has never been any pretence even of comprehensive enforcement. In practical terms this is simply not possible. The factor of discretion cannot be sufficiently emphasised. The law is designed to enable peace to be preserved and to achieve this it is necessarily widely drawn. It is made workable and indeed acceptable in a civilised society solely by the factor of discretion. Indeed for the vast majority of people the fact of a particular law's existence is a matter of no concern. What matters is the law in practice, for it is the law as activated by the police, by the prosecutors and by the courts which defines the extent of our liberty at any one time. If we look back to the successful campaign to repeal the old 'sus' law (section 4 of the Vagrancy Act 1824), it centred on the question of the operation of that law. Most people would acknowledge that there are occasions where a power to take persons into custody is necessary, even if no substantive crime has been committed or attempted, but many people were unhappy about the way the discretion to arrest, i.e. to activate the law, was being exercised. It did little justice to the arguments of the reformers for the defence of the 'sus' law to be based on a need for such law, without acknowledging the difficulties of its operation.[8]

The factor of discretion has both beneficial elements and elements of difficulty. It would obviously be intolerable if the laws which preserve public order and tranquillity were used to bring about a state of total quietism. It is the element of discretion which should safeguard against this, while still retaining the availability of the law in appropriate circumstances. A second beneficial aspect is that the factor of discretion does allow the law in operation to differentiate between classes or categories of disorder for which the bare statement of the common law or mere wording of a statute does not make provision. The alternative aspect of discretion is that in the public order field many different views may honourably and even reasonably be held as to how discretion should be exercised. It is thus inescapable that almost any exercise of discretion will provoke feelings both of approval and of disapproval. Perhaps this can be well illustrated by a consideration of a recent and well publicised event in the autumn of 1985.[9]

Mr. Ian Botham, while on a sponsored walk from John o' Groats to Land's End, was reported to have struck a police constable who was shepherding the party of walkers to one side of the road to allow free passage of traffic on the other side – an example of balance as described by Lord Scarman. To some it may appear to have been a trivial matter, not worthy of attention, indeed nothing more than the sort of thing which happens when human beings, tired, sincere and perhaps anxious, are placed in a tense but essentially human situation. In other words this was an event which could be brought within our current notions of an ordered society and no intervention by the agencies of the law would be required. However, in an alternative view, this was a public display of force, or minor act of violence by one citizen perpetrated on another, which could be seen as rocking one of the pillars of the state, its impact further compounded by the fact that Mr. Botham is a public figure, the object of much hero worship by young and not so young members of our society. In this view, therefore, the law should take a hand in the proceedings. The range of opinion is by no means exhausted by these two views. For some people the circumstances of the whole affair, the one disorderly incident in a lengthy act of charity would entitle Mr. Botham's conduct to be viewed with such benevolence as would deny the necessity for the law to get involved. The policeman was reported merely to have expressed disappointment and to have taken no action.

Let us now change the facts a little. What if a group of people, unconventional both in dress and hairstyle, march down the street carrying placards and shouting slogans which advocate a change in the law to remove all criminal sanctions against adults who have sexual intercourse with children. One of their number pushes aside a police officer who is shepherding them to one side of the road to facilitate the free movement of traffic. To some, such a cause and perhaps such people are not worthy of any official benevolence. To others, because the act is in the context of a political statement and a contribution to the democratic evolution of our society, then, regardless of whether any particular views that the marchers advocate are considered to be good or bad, a benevolent view is appropriate.

The important point to be made is that the law can only be enforced on a discretionary basis. Laws on public order are not self-activating: they rely on a view being formed by human actors both as to what constitutes order and disorder and also as to how a particular act should be characterised. It is by no means surprising to find that a whole chapter in what is still one of the leading texts on public order is entitled 'The Policeman on the Spot'.[10] In many public order cases the only evidence for the prosecution is provided by the policeman, frequently policeman/victim, on the spot. This is particularly so of offences under the Public Order Act 1936, section 5 and under the Police Act 1964, section 51(3). The National Council for Civil Liberties Inquiry into the Policing of the Miners' Strike went further as follows:

> Police powers in the street and places of public resort are, in practice, considerable, since police officers themselves effectively make the definitions of offensive behaviour under the Public Order Act 1936 and of obstruction under the Police Act 1964 through their decisions whether to make an arrest.[11]

## INDIVIDUALS AND GROUPS

Before we end our initial considerations there is one further aspect which we must acknowledge. Again a rugby analogy provides an appropriate starting point. On occasions when a violent encounter is anticipated players have sometimes homogenised their team to prevent individuals being picked out by opponents. At times the plan has evolved further so that if one of their number is in difficulty the whole team will come to his aid. The thinking here is that if an individual player can be identified perpetrating a violent act on an opponent he risks being sent off – a possible outcome – or being victimised by the opposing players – a probable outcome. However if all the players are involved the risk is merely that the whole game will be abandoned by the referee, in practical terms a most unlikely outcome We would all agree that the referee is placed in a situation of great difficulty in such circumstances; he neither has the appropriate tools, i.e. the rules of the game, to punish, nor the manpower to prevent such conduct. That situation resembles the legal dilemma in relation to public disorder.

The criminal law is geared entirely towards the prosecution of individual offenders for their own acts insofar as this can be proved to the satisfaction of a bench of magistrates or of a jury. The individual must be identified, the act in question must be shown to have been clearly his, any necessary mental elements must be proved, e.g. intention, and the whole must be clearly demonstrated to the court's satisfaction to fall squarely within the ambit of a particular crime as defined by the common law or by statute. This is wholly inappropriate where there is obvious public disorder caused by large numbers of participants. To wait for a particular criminal act to be done or even attempted is frequently to court disaster. To identify a particular individual as the one who threw the brick is practically impossible in many cases. To affix a mental element on a large group of individuals is by no means an easy matter. Many of the major crimes, riot and unlawful assembly to name but two, cry out for a modern redefinition. Perhaps for these reasons the laws relating to public order tend to be less than precise and certainly have at times been treated as such by the courts (see for example *Thomas* v *Sawkins*, 1935).[11a] Some are of a different character from the generality of crimes in that they enable participation in group activity to be punished. Lastly they recognise that powers of prevention are equally important as laws which punish conduct. With these matters in mind let us move to consider the laws and their operation.

## THE LAW: SUBSTANTIVE CRIMES[12]

In this section we will survey the various crimes which may be committed by those engaged in violent conduct or who threaten to cause disorder in the public domain. First, it is an offence under the Public Order Act 1936, section 2, for anyone to organise others to usurp the functions of either the police or the armed forces, and it is also an offence to organise others for the use or display of physical force in promoting any political object. Essentially this provision was introduced to enable the law to deal with private armies. It is an orthodox criminal provision requiring proof of individual conduct. The issue may be tried either before magistrates or before a judge and jury, but all prosecutions must be approved by the Attorney General. This section is cearly directed against violence and force. Meeting together to petition the government of the day for the redress of grievances is a necessary freedom in any democratic society. In America it is safeguarded by the First Amendment to the Constitution. It is the violent methods which command the attention of the law. Violence and force are essentially policing issues. It is therefore unfortunate that the Attorney General is tied into the prosecution process. He is an officer of state who, although independent of the government of the day, is by no means distanced from it. Prosecutions have been brought against members of 'Spearhead', a branch of the British National Party (1963), members of the 'Free Wales Army' (1969) and members of the Irish Republican Army (1984).[13] It will be noted that a considerable degree of organisation is, or was, present in each of these three bodies and the section would appear to be inappropriate for use against ad hoc groups. Significantly, groups of stewards employed to keep order at public meetings are excluded from these provisions (see section 2(3)).

There are other provisions specifically directed against organisers. The Sedition Meetings Act 1817, section 23, makes it an offence to call together 50 or more persons for the purpose of a demonstration or meeting within one mile of the Houses of Parliament. Here is a relatively early example of the law being concerned with 'mass' demonstrations, it focuses on numbers and the intimidation or disorder that numbers can create. Again the section is an orthodox, criminal one directed against the act of convening such a meeting. If this preventative measure fails and the meeting assembles the section goes on to provide that anyone who participates does so in an unlawful assembly.

We now move from a consideration of organisational offences to a consideration of the legal rules which relate to violent conduct itself. It is immediately apparent that the law lacks that precision which we might expect to find in, for example, the law of contract or the law of trusts. In part this must be a result of the law in this field having scarcely been visited by the Court of Appeal and the House of Lords. The vast majority of the offences which we are to consider are tried before magistrates. This facilitates the speedy and effective processing of many individual defendants after an outbreak of disorder. The speedy visitation of retribution may well be one way of curtailing disorder. When we come to consider the major common law offences of riot and unlawful assembly we find that they can only be tried on indictment, before judge and jury. This is only right given the serious nature of the charges and the likelihood of heavy penalties on conviction. But the process is a slow one which may hamper the immediate resolution of disorder, for it may well result in those involved in the disorder being returned, albeit perhaps temporarily, to the heart of the disorder, or else in unnecessary and punitive remands in custody or bail on oppressive conditions.

A criminal breach of the peace seems to be some act or course of conduct which involves either actual harm to a person or his property in his presence or else puts somebody in fear of such harm being done. Something more than a mere disturbance is required, an essential element is violence (see *R v Howell (Erroll)*, 1982).[14] Both the ordinary citizen and the citizen policeman have a duty to put an end to a breach of the peace which is actually occurring and to prevent a breach of the peace which they reasonably believe to be about to happen. This duty is unenforceable against an ordinary citizen, i.e. a duty of imperfect obligation (see *Albert v Lavin*, 1982).[15] All reasonable steps may be taken to prevent a breach of the peace, this power is retained by the Police and Criminal Evidence Act 1984, section 26.

It is on the above concept that many offences relating to violence and disorder are based. The most widely utilised – so much so that at times it has appeared a catch-all – is, of course, the Public Order Act 1936, section 5. In exceptionally precise language for this area of the law, it creates a summary offence, triable only before magistrates, of using threatening, abusive or insulting words or behaviour in a public place with intent to provoke a breach of the peace or whereby a breach of the peace is likely to be occasioned. In many ways this is the key weapon against disorder. The police have a power of arrest under section 7 of the same Act which thus enables them to remove troublemakers from the scene of the action. It is unnecessary to prove that the person arrested actually caused a breach of the peace, it is sufficient if one is occasioned and a connection established between the conduct or words and the disorder. The precise meaning of the offence as drafted seems clear enough. There must be a breach of the peace – or at least the likelihood of one – and the behaviour must go beyond that which is merely offensive or annoying (see *Brutus* v *Cozens*, 1973).[16] In *Hudson* v *Chief Constable of Avon and Somerset* (1976)[17] H. was an over-excited football supporter who in his excited state fell forward and by creating a domino effect in the crowd caused a crowd surge. His conduct was found by the Queen's Bench Divisional Court not to constitute the offence – the opposite view to that taken by the magistrates. However in practice the courts have frequently taken a somewhat relaxed view as to what constitutes the offence: in some cases if a breach of the peace occurs then it seems to follow that the behaviour inevitably is found to fall within the definition; in others anti-social conduct has been brought within the offence simply because of its nature rather than because a breach of the peace is likely. It should be noted that the Queen's Bench Divisional Court has taken a more literal line in recent years (see *Marsh* v *Arscott*[18] and *Parkin* v *Norman*,[19] both 1982).

It must not be forgotten that section 5 creates an orthodox criminal offence which requires specific proof of individual guilt, yet it has considerable utility in facilitating the arrest of a trouble-maker, for such an arrest need only be made on reasonable suspicion that the offence is being committed. Reasonable suspicion is an elusive concept – so much so that the Royal Commission on Criminal Procedure in 1981[20] felt that it would be impracticable to provide a statutory definition. Instead it sought to prevent random action by recommending procedural safe-guards, for example notifying reasons, making records. The courts have shown no greater willingness to hamper the police with technical definitions on this point. The courts view reason-able suspicion as a bona fide state of conjecture which may be a long way from actual proof. In short they seem to be willing to accept almost any suspicion as reasonable, only intervening where there is such evidence of perversity as will undermine the notion of a suspicion.[21]

Despite the foregoing, section 5 has been criticised on the grounds that it is inadequate with regard to obtaining con-victions. In his evidence to Lord Scarman's Inquiry into the Brixton Disorders in 1981,[22] the then Metropolitan Police Commissioner claimed that section 5 was inadequate to meet the problem of disorder because in such circumstances it may be impossible to prove that a particular individual was acting in a particular way. Lord Scarman was not persuaded by this criticism. Furthermore, in his evidence the Commissioner referred to the primary task of quelling disorder – this can be achieved by using the arrest powers annexed to section 5, it does not necessarily require a successful prosecution at some, perhaps distant, time in the future.

Recently several crimes, no so long ago thought to be obsolete, have been revived in relation to public disorder and violence. In general terms if three or more people are gathered together for a common purpose either to commit a crime of violence or for some other object, which need not be an unlawful one, in such a way as to cause a reasonable man to apprehend a breach of the peace, then they constitute an unlawful assembly. As soon as they do some act towards the execution of their common purpose then they constitute a rout. As soon as the group actually executes, even if in part only, its common purpose then this constitutes a riot. In reality all three are part of the same spectrum, and the elusive place of rout has meant that it is no longer prosecuted. All three are common law offences, triable before a judge and jury and which carry a potential maximum penalty of life imprisonment.

If we consider first unlawful assembly, we find that it is scarcely defined with precision. In essence the crime consists of grouping together or even just being in a group with a specific common state of mind. At first sight it would appear a difficult crime to establish to a court's satisfaction, since the prosecution must establish that the individuals gathered together intend to use or abet the use of violence or to do or abet acts which they know to be likely to cause a breach of the peace. However, because it is inextricably linked to the notion of breach of the peace, it does provide a power of arrest and thus a means for the police to remove a group from the heart of the disorder. The crime of unlawful assembly has been successfully used to prosecute pickets who intimidate those going to work – see *R* v *Jones* (1974),[23] the Shrewsbury pickets case – and against students demonstrating in a foreign embassy (*Kamara* v *D.P.P.*, 1974).[24]

The leading case, *Beatty* v *Gilbanks*,[25] is rather unsatisfactory. In 1882 B and others, all members of the Salvation Army, marched through the streets of Weston-super-Mare. Suffice it for our purposes to say that violence in the streets was both foreseeable and foreseen; indeed the local magistrates purported to ban such a march. Salvation Army marches at that time were noisy affairs: they tended to collect a mob along the route, frequently the marchers were met by the Skeleton Army, ad hoc groups of intoxicated ruffians bent on disrupting the march, and on many occasions the whole degenerated into a general fight. The police were frequently unable to cope. After being bound over to keep the peace, B appealed to the Divisional Court on the basis that a bind over was only possible if he had done something which constituted a criminal offence. The court accepted that that was indeed the state of the law then (it is not so now) and considered whether B was guilty of unlawful assembly. It decided not. The activities of the Salvation Army were lawful in themselves and no specific blame was attached to them, notwithstanding that violence occurred and would not have occurred without their presence.

If however the court feels able to characterise conduct as 'provocative' and disorder ensues, then the offence of unlawful assembly may be established, an interpretation of *Wise* v *Dunning* (1902).[26] The law is by no means clear and few cases have reached even the Divisional Court. Almost everything will depend on an interpretation of facts. It is not surprising that charges under the Public Order Act 1936, section 5, tend to be preferred to those for unlawful assembly; the former are triable before magistrates, and thus justice tends to be speedier and the issue of proof less complex than for unlawful assembly.

Riot has an archaic flavour and is rightly considered to be a serious offence. After a lean period, charges of riot have been laid more frequently since the early 1960s. Charges of riotous assembly were successfully prosecuted against student demonstrators who invaded a hotel in Cambridge (*R* v *Caird*, 1970),[27] against prisoners who rioted at Parkhurst Prison (*R* v *Anderson*, 1970)[28] and against rampaging spectators at a motorcycle race meeting (*R* v *Hevans*, 1979).[29] Most recently publicity has centred around spectacular and unsuccessful prosecutions for riot arising out of the St. Paul's disorders in Bristol in 1980, and of activities during the recent miners' strike of 1984/5.

The difficulties involved in proving charges of riot are not insignificant. The criminal law requires specific proof against each individual in relation to the elements of the crime. There are five elements in the crime, namely three or more persons gathered together for a common purpose who at least partially execute their purpose, intending to help each other by force, if necessary, against anyone who may oppose them, and such force or violence must be such as to alarm at least one other person present who is of reasonable firmness and courage. The Riot (Damages) Act 1886 allows those who have suffered at the hands of rioters to seek compensation out of the local police funds. The Act is statutory acknowledgement that it is the police and no longer the local inhabitants who are responsible for keeping order in the locality.

The trial arising out of the St. Paul's disorders[30] took seven weeks at a cost of £500,000; three of the 16 defendants were acquitted by direction of the judge, five acquitted by the jury and the jury failed to agree a verdict on the remainder. The trial took place long after the disorders. The jury appear to have taken the matter of proof very seriously, indeed the aura of the charge may have counted against the prosecution.[31] The Director of Public Prosecutions subsequently expressed the view that it had perhaps been a mistake to bring such charges.

The remaining common law crime which plays a significant part in the preservation of order is that of affray. Put simply, this constitutes unlawful fighting or violence in circumstances where a reasonably stout-hearted bystander might be put in terror. Again it is a crime with a recent history after a period of desuetude. It is a crime to which the authorities can resort where the fighting is such that evidence sufficient to convict any one individual for assault is not available (see *Button* v *Director of Public Prosecutions*, 1966).[32] In its revived form the offence is essentially concerned with actual violence, not simply terrorising others (see *Taylor* v *Director of Public Prosecutions*, 1973).[33]

The courts have indicated that affray is a serious criminal charge, not lightly to be resorted to by prosecutors (see *R* v *Crimlis*, 1976).[34] It is certainly easier to prove affray than it is to establish several other offences: no common purpose is necessary, it is not necessary to establish who did what, nor is it

necessary for anyone actually to have been terrorised. The range
of sentence extends to life imprisonment so there is ample scope
for exemplary punishment. The norm is for a custodial sentence
to be deemed appropriate. However it must be seen in context. It
is essentially a weapon for dealing with short sharp outbreaks of
violent disorder, e.g. spontaneous fights at dance halls, gang
fights, fighting at football matches. Its utility lies in its deterrent
effects – and thus it is not surprising to find its recent revival in
the minds of prosecutors. Nonetheless Williams[35] does rightly
question whether prosecutors should be free to revive old crimes
at their convenience. There comes a time when such resuscitation
should be left to Parliament, for that body to redefine archaic
crimes in modern terms. The same comments could equally
apply to the archaic offence of 'watching and besetting', under
the Conspiracy and Protection of Property Act, 1875, section 7,
which was recently resorted to during the miners' strike of
1984/5.

It will thus be seen that the criminal laws which touch directly
upon public violence and disorder are scarcely adequate. The
notion that future public disorder can be prevented by the ex post
facto bringing of orthodox criminal charges or by the threat that
at some time in the future a deterrent sentence may be given to
those responsible for disorder is scarcely tenable. The offences
are essentially punitive. In any case, if disorder actually occurs
the orthodox criminal law may simply be unable to be utilised.
For example, at the outset of the St. Paul's riots in Bristol in 1980
the police had to withdraw initially to await further resources.
Furthermore if disorder breaks out the police will have a pre-
eminent task of restoring order as soon as possible. The apprehension of criminals exists only within the framework of this
prime objective. There is a further danger in disordered circumstances that an attempt to enforce the criminal law will actually
fuel the disorder. Even after an arrest and charge, the use of the
orthodox criminal law may not result in a conviction. This is
doubly dangerous. The police on the one hand may feel that they
have not been given the support they are entitled to expect either
from the law or from the courts. The public on the other hand may
well gain the impression that the police have been haphazard or
even perverse in the enforcement of the law. Finally, if the

criminal law runs its course and a deterrent sentence is visited upon those responsible it will be visited upon them many months later and in an atmosphere of calm and order. There is a danger that such sentences will be viewed in the context of the ordered society in which they are given, rather than the disordered time when the criminal acts took place. In such a light they may be hard to justify to those not involved in the disorder and may even seem barbaric.

The sad truth is, however, that disorder is itself an example of failure. Ex post facto measures to deal with disorder are nothing more than putting water on a fire which has already begun. The trick is to prevent the fire in the first place. Just as with a fire, which from the moment of its inception causes damage, so too with disorder. Any breakdown in public order in our ordered society damages at least the social fabric of society. For this reason the law has provided a battery of preventative measures to assist the police and others in preventing disorder.

## THE LAWS OF PREVENTION[36]

If we return to the Inquiry by Lord Scarman into the Red Lion Square Disorders[37] and in particular to the evidence of the then Metropolitan Police Commissioner, Sir Robert Mark, an important point emerges. He was of the view that in general people tend to avoid extreme violence. He also indicated that the general police practice has been to favour a policy of containment. The two in reality go hand in hand. Containment is only possible if the activities involved cause no more than minor dislocation to public life. It depends on the availability of adequate police resources. It is only possible where the dislocation or disorderliness can be brought within the acceptable bounds of an ordered society. Containment also depends to a great degree on a willingness of those on the streets, be they demonstrating, picketing or celebrating a football victory, to seek a limited objective, whether that be the presentation of a point of view or something else. At all events their objective must fall short of confrontation either with the police or with their opponents. There must also exist an element of mutual goodwill between the police and those on the streets. The demonstrators must exhibit a willingness to be contained. The police must not by their actions entirely frustrate the limited objectives of those demonstrating, picketing or whatever. They must enable them to achieve their aim of putting forward a point of view. In fact, in the vast majority of instances the citizen and the police work well and closely together, each seeking and attaining their respective goals of putting forward a point of view and of maintaining order. It is not the norm, nor has it been, for people in the streets to arm themselves in any way. The police have achieved their objectives of containment without recourse to equipment, whether offensive or defensive, beyond the normal police issue of truncheon and uniform. It is when this mutuality breaks down that there is a great danger of violence and disorder. Some citizens take to the public stage with a prime objective of confrontation and are unwilling to acquiesce in being contained within a lesser objective. If the police cannot bring about continuing order by their mere presence, fortified by their having recourse to the orthodox criminal law, then preventative policing by other methods is called for. In this area of life preventative powers allocated to the authorities have been far greater than in any other sphere of activity.

The police have powers under the Public Order Act 1936, section 3 to control demonstrations where they reasonably apprehend 'serious public disorder'. On one analysis (see for example the Court of Appeal in *R* v *Chief Constable of Devon and Cornwall ex p C.E.G.B.*, 1982),[38] any public disorder is, ipso facto, serious. It may be, however, that these police powers are only to be used when the disorder anticipated is above and beyond the social dislocation inevitably caused by a large group of people, moving en masse, probably vociferous and certainly intent on giving an impression of forceful association. The police are given exceedingly wide powers to issue directions and may even apply to the local authority, or the Home Secretary if within the Metropolitan area, for an order banning all or any class of processions. These are very wide preventative powers and any conduct in defiance will constitute either an offence of obstructing a police officer in the execution of his duty or the substantive offence under section 3(4) of organising a prohibited demonstration. The points to note are, first, that the police powers are very wide, it merely being required that the police officer has 'reasonable grounds' for apprehending serious public disorder. Second, it matters not who might cause the disorder, it is sufficient that disorder is apprehended. Third, the attempt to insulate the police from the consequences of a 'political' decision is largely illusory. No responsible local authority or Home Secretary could go against the opinion of the local chief officer of police.

Here is a clear attempt to combat disorder before it arises. The focus is on disorder and the niceties of the criminal law as generally operated do not apply. It is possible under section 3 to criminalise otherwise lawful conduct at the behest of the police officer on the spot. That decision cannot be taken in a detached way but must be made either in the heat of the moment, if the march is already in being, or with anticipation of serious disorder. It is of course possible that this criminalisation of otherwise lawful conduct may produce violent reaction. It is not at present necessary in all cases to give the police prior warning of a demonstration. This largely depends on local acts of parliament, for example the East Sussex Act 1891, section 29 requires 48 hours' notice to the police. Lord Scarman in his Report on the Red Lion Square Disorders felt that there was no need for notice in all cases, acknowledging the value of a spontaneous demonstration. (He found that in 80 per cent of cases notice was given.) The workable nature of the law relies on containment being practicable within the constraints of police resources, particularly manpower. Serious problems arise when police resources are stretched or when the marchers are hell-bent on not being contained. It is still the case that some large groups cannot afford to meet elsewhere than in the streets. In addition violence is essentially newsworthy – it is possible for a group to achieve vast media coverage, out of all proportion to the numbers involved, if the violence is newsworthy. There are thus tensions at work which suggest that policies of containment may not always succeed.

One may argue that violent protest, since it is a contribution to the democratic process and feeds into the evolutionary development of our society, should be treated more favourably. However, viewed from the perspective of the violent act, it matters little whether the disorder is caused by football hooligans, by pickets or by political demonstrators. It is the case that the law does not differentiate – such activity is characterised as violence (see *R* v *Caird*, 1970)[39] and thus simply criminal.

The law rightly offers protection for a policeman who is carrying out his duty. It is thus an aggravated crime to assault a police officer in the execution of his duty – see the Police Act 1964, section 51(1). It is also an offence to obstruct a police officer in the execution of his duty under section 51(3). It is difficult to be dogmatic about the extent of a police officer's duties;[40] suffice it for our purposes to state that his primary duties are to preserve the peace and to prevent crime. The courts have been conspicuous in not further defining the police officer's duties. In *Coffin* v *Smith* (1980)[41] Lord Justice Donaldson declined to 'reduce within specific limits the general terms in which the duties of police constables have been expressed'. The approach which he favoured was, first, to consider whether what the officer in question was doing fell broadly within the general scope of his duties. If it did, then the officer's exercise of powers could only be upset if they were found to be clearly unjustified. On this view the onus is on those questioning the actions of the police officer to establish either that his conduct fell outside his duties or else he abused his powers, for example, by using excessive force. Once we recall the nature of those general duties – to preserve the peace and to prevent crime – it is unlikely that the courts will adopt a restrictive attitude to police conduct so long as there is a bona fide link between what the policeman is doing and the preservation of law and order or prevention of crime. This will be particularly so if there is a patent threat to the public peace or if disorder has already broken out.

However, even if we accept that a policeman's duties are to be widely drawn and that his powers to fulfil his duties should not be unduly restricted, there is an obverse to consider. The typical use of police powers to prevent a breach of the peace include the following: the separation of rival groups of fans going to and from a football match; giving directions to marchers under the Public Order Act 1936, section 3; controlling the number of pickets at factory gates; ordering a speaker to desist where disorder is threatened. In each of these instances, one or more of the fundamental liberties which are inextricably part of an ordered, as opposed to an oppressed, society will at best be modified, at worst overridden. It is possible that freedom of speech, of movement and even of association will be at issue. These are matters about which many people have very firmly held views. There is also today a widespread readiness to question authority, to seek some justification for the policeman's action or instruction beyond the mere fact that he believes it is necessary to preserve the peace or prevent crime. The fact that to obey the police officer's instructions may mean that the individual citizen is being asked to abandon his pursuit of a specific goal, whether it be to picket, to demonstrate or noisily to extol the merits of his favoured football team, will frequently add to the tension of the situation.

In many instances of public disorder there are two or more factions. It is neither necessary for the preservation of order, nor may it be possible in practice, to exercise control over each one in order to preserve the peace. This will not endear the police officer to those of the particular faction to whom instructions are given or on whom restrictions are placed. At best the whole may degenerate into a verbal attack on the police, at worst this may result in overreaction. The fact that to preserve the peace inevitably touches adversely on other people's liberties means that this is inevitable. In an already tense situation any failure to obey the police officer, be it only a temporary or a partial failure, will contribute to disorder.

It must never be forgotten that keeping the peace is a balancing process.[42] That process is not best achieved in a tense and public atmosphere. It is also inhibited by such mundane considerations as the practicalities of policing: are there sufficient police available to allow a speaker to address a crowd, should demonstrators be stopped before they reach their destinations because there are inadequate resources to police the demonstration itself?

The whole issue is clouded because of an inherent dualism in the law. The law gives wide powers to the police to enable them to carry out their duties, especially to preserve the peace. These wide powers may involve limiting the freedom of others in order to preserve order. The limitation of the freedoms of others is justified not because what they are doing is intrinsically an abuse of those freedoms, i.e. a criminal act, but simply in order to preserve the peace in a situation where violence and disorder are reasonably apprehended. Yet notwithstanding the non-criminal nature of the exercise of liberty, any failure to obey the police officer's instructions will be an obstruction of the police officer in the exercise of his duty, i.e. a criminal offence contrary to the Police Act 1964, section 51(3). In other words the exercise of discretion by the police officer may result in the criminalisation of non-criminal conduct. This is the great danger inherent in preventative powers. So long as they are uncontested all is well. As soon as there is a breakdown in the relationship between the police officer and the citizen, either because of lack of mutual confidence or because the one has in mind a goal which can only be attained by the frustration of the other's objective, the issue of a sanction looms large. That sanction is provided by criminal law, that part of the law which normally requires specific individual proof that a particular individual has himself done an act in a particular state of mind which is contrary to pre-ordained and knowable rules. It is for these reasons that preventative powers can on the one hand be an aid to preserving law and order and yet can also appear to contribute to the breakdown of order.

It is necessary neither for an actual crime to have been committed nor, if a crime is committed, for the individual who is the subject of the police officer's instructions to be reasonably suspected of an offence. It is sufficient for the officer to reasonably suspect a breach of the peace. The courts in fact do not closely scrutinise police action; there is almost a presumption that the police view is reasonable unless it can be shown that the police officer is acting perversely. There is no need for any physical obstruction of the police officer, it is sufficient merely to make his job more difficult. The problem is of course that once the police officer has decided to act the citizen has little alternative but to comply. Yet the police command has the effect of creating a legal obligation to obey where there is no other lawful duty to do so vested by statute or by common law. The public order context and in particular the apprehension of a breach of the peace is doubly important. First, it is the justification for the police officer using his preventative powers. Second, although – somewhat incongruously – there is no power of arrest for merely obstructing a police officer in the exercise of his duty, the apprehension of a breach of the peace will justify arrest.

A full appreciation of the vast nature of preventative powers can perhaps be gleaned from the following examples. A police officer who reasonably apprehended public disorder if H continued to wear an orange lily, a sectarian emblem, while walking in the street, was held entitled to remove the lily upon her refusal to do (*Humphries* v *Connor*, 1864).[43] Presumably her refusal to remove the lily would equally constitute an offence of obstruction. The police may forbid a meeting if they reasonably apprehend a breach of the peace (see *O'Kelly* v *Harvey*, 1883).[44] A speaker may be asked to stop speaking or even to go elsewhere if disorder is anticipated, even if this is only amongst the audience (*Duncan* v *Jones*, 1936).[45] The police can regulate the number of pickets at factory gates (see *Piddington* v *Bates*, 1960).[46]

A police officer can ask a member of the public who pushed to the front of a queue to board a bus to stand aside in a shop doorway and enter the bus only after the others had boarded (see *Albert* v *Lavin*, 1982).[47] Presumably any refusal to comply would constitute the offence of obstruction, since the police officer reasonably apprehended a breach of the peace if he did not intervene. The Police and Criminal Evidence Act 1984, section 25, has added a power of arrest where a police officer reasonably suspects that any offence has been committed. The person suspected may be arrested if one of the general arrest conditions set out in section 25(3) is fulfilled. The first of these conditions is that 'the name of the relevant person is unknown to, and cannot be readily ascertained by, the constable'. Thus one who merely obstructs a police officer in the execution of his duty, which is not an arrestable offence (see *Gelberg* v *Miller*, 1961)[48] may be arrested if he cannot provide satisfactory proof of his identity, regardless of whether a breach of the peace is reasonably apprehended.

The breadth of these powers has not gone without criticism. In *Humphries* v *Connor* the court referred to a notion of necessity – the policeman's action had to be necessary – but this has not been taken by the courts to mean that it must be of last resort. The courts have merely required that the apprehension be based on evidence which in reason could support the conclusion that a breach of the peace was more than a remote possibility (see *Piddington* v *Bates*). Thus all will turn on the facts of each case. The initial interpretation is that of the police officer. In a majority of cases the only evidence for the prosecution will be that of the police officer present on the spot. The courts are unwilling to intervene. Indeed they have given the impression that the police officer's view should be supported unless it is wholly unreasonable; thus Lord Chief Justice Parker stated, in *Piddington* v *Bates*:[49] 'I think that a police officer charged with the duty of preserving the Queen's peace must be left to take such steps as on the evidence before him he thinks proper.' Put shortly, the courts will not risk undermining the powers of the police to preserve peace and good order by any undue or excessive concern for legal niceties.

Preventative powers do not reside solely with the police. The courts have wide powers to bind over members of the public either 'to keep the peace', where there is a reasonable apprehension of 'personal danger', or 'to be of good behaviour', where the activities of members of the public give rise to the apprehension that a breach of the peace is a probable consequence.[50] These powers are of ancient origin and have frequently been utilised to combat disorder. There is no need for a criminal conviction before an order is made. In technical terms a 'bind over' is not a conviction, but may appear so in all but nature. Anyone who refuses to be bound over, who cannot find securities or who is in default of the conditions risks a term of imprisonment. There is little to differentiate a fine and loss of surety viewed from the perspective of the person who is bound over and who is subsequently in default. Both involve separating a man and his money.

The circumstances in which such an order can be made are very wide indeed and conspicuously ill-defined. This 'aura of vagueness' has been described as an 'asset to prosecutors'.[51]

The orders are deterrent in quality and, as with the preventative powers of the police, have the effect of imposing duties and sanctions on individual citizens beyond those which are imposed upon the generality of members of the public.


THE LAW: PROPOSED REFORMS

Following proposals made by the Law Commission in 1983,[52] and in the aftermath of recent serious disorders, the Home Secretary has introduced into Parliament a new Public Order Bill.[53] The most important provisions for the purposes of this essay are to be found in Parts I and II, respectively, creating new statutory offences to replace the old common law ones of riot, unlawful assembly and affray (see clause 9), and revising the laws relating to processions and assemblies.

Clause 1 creates a new statutory offence of riot. If 12 or more people are present together or threaten violence for a common purpose, and if their collective conduct is such as would cause a person of reasonable firmness to fear for his personal safety, then each member of the group will be guilty of riot. It is a clear attempt to criminalise group activity, but clause 6 emphasises that the prosecution must prove intention on the part of each individual to use violence or at least awareness that his conduct may be violent. The law avails the prosecutor to the extent that the common purpose can be inferred from conduct and that no other person need be present at the scene. It would appear thus that in many cases the only evidence available to the prosecution will be that of the arresting officer, who forms a view of the character of the group's conduct. The offence is a very serious one, triable on indictment alone. It carries a maximum penalty of life imprisonment. The consent of the Director of Public Prosecutions is necessary for all prosecutions under this clause.

Clause 2, violent disorder, is the new statutory version of the old unlawful assembly. The crime is essentially the same as for riot under clause 1 except that the group need only be three or more and there is no necessity for a common purpose. It thus covers violent conduct not designed to achieve a specific end. The new offence is triable either by magistrates or by judge and jury. In the latter case the penalty is up to a maximum of five years' imprisonment. The essence of the offence is violent collective conduct; the offence will still be committed if, for example, the three members of the group individually take it in turns to throw bricks at rival football supporters.

Clause 3 replaces the old law of affray. The new offence is aimed at individual conduct. It is committed if violence is used or threatened towards another, and if the conduct would cause a person of reasonable firmness if present, which need not be the case, to fear for his personal safety. It is not sufficient merely to

threaten with words. The offence is triable either before
magistrates or a judge and jury; in the latter case the penalty is up
to three years' imprisonment. Significantly the police are given a
power of arrest where it is reasonably suspected that someone is
committing the offence. If the constable merely apprehends the
commission of the offence he can presumably rely on his powers
to prevent a breach of the peace to make an arrest. The old
provisions relating to threatening or provocative words or
behaviour, section 5 of the Public Order Act 1936, are largely
reproduced in the new bill, clause 4. The former verbiage –
'threatening, abusive, or insulting' – is retained. The new bill (see
clause 7) makes it clear that the offences mentioned above are
part of one spectrum. Thus a defendant charged under clause 1
can be acquitted of that charge but found guilty of one of the
lesser offences.

A new offence of disorderliness or hooliganism is created by
clause 5. It is wider than the old section 5 of the Public Order Act
1936 in that it covers 'disorderly' behaviour as well as threatening,
abusive or insulting behaviour, and it is sufficient if the defendant
reasonably believes that his words or conduct are likely to harass,
alarm or distress another who would appear to have to be present
or at least 'available' to be harassed, alarmed or distressed. A
police officer may arrest without warrant one whom he suspects
of being guilty of the offence and who after a warning persists in
engaging in offensive conduct. The offence is triable only before
magistrates.

It cannot be claimed that these new provisions go much further
than making marginal adjustments to the law. The problems
associated with the major crimes may be to some extent
alleviated. However the new offences under clauses 4 and 5
retain the catch-all qualities of their forerunners and little has
been done to clarify exactly what they cover. Much will still turn
on the exercise of discretion by the policeman on the spot.

The old law on processions and marches, section 3 of the Public
Order Act 1936, is largely reproduced, with additions, in Part II,
but significant changes are made. Clause 11 now requires advance
notice of public processions to be given to the local police at least
six days before the intended procession. The powers which the
police formerly had to impose conditions which appear necessary

to prevent serious public disorder are now widened to include the prevention of serious damage to property or serious disruption to the life of the community. Conditions may further be imposed if the procession is organised with a view to intimidating others in order to compel the latter either to do an act which they have a right not to do or not to do an act which they have a right to do. It would thus appear to cover a mass procession in support of a static picket. The new bill makes failing to adhere to conditions imposed by the police a substantive offence, not, as formerly, a possible obstruction of a police officer under the Police Act 1964, section 51(3). There is also a power of arrest available to a police officer who suspects that an offence under this clause is being committed. It will be apparent that the preventative powers available to the police are now more widely drawn in relation to marches than they were before. Clause 13 retains the pre-emptive power to ban public processions if serious public disorder cannot be averted by the use of the preventative powers in clause 12.

The preventative powers formerly applied to marches and demonstrations are to be extended by clause 14 to static public assemblies. Again the concern with numbers looms large, and the spectre of mass pickets cannot have been far from the draftsman's mind. The police may impose conditions on static assemblies in the same way as for processions; these may include conditions as to place, duration and as to numbers if they appear necessary to prevent serious disorder, damage, disruption or intimidation. There appears no power to impose conditions as to timing. It is a criminal offence to participate in a public assembly and fail to comply with conditions imposed by the police.

Clearly Part II confers major new preventative powers on the police. It is a recognition that the presence of a large group can be a threat to an ordered society, and that the policing of such groups once they have come into existence in the modern climate of affairs is exceedingly difficult, if not impossible, in many cases.

THE LAW: PRACTICALITIES

Above we have dealt with the major, specific and less than specific legal powers available to the police to enable them to

preserve peace and order. It will be readily apparent that they are
both potent and at the same time limited. These powers are
available to deal with disorder but cannot be said to be the answer
to a widespread breakdown in order. When the level of violence
and disorder in society extends beyond a particular threshold
many tensions will begin to operate. This suggests that practical
demands will ensure that the margins and hinterland of both the
law and legalism are explored. The law relating to public order is
inevitably a response to notions of disorder. The practice of
policing disorder relates inevitably to experiences of disorder. It
is no surprise therefore to find that changes in the law tend to be in
response to particular situations: the Public Order Act 1936 was a
response to the fascist disorder of the early 1930s; the resurrection
of the old crime of affray coincided with the activities of 'mods'
and 'rockers'. This has led to claims that the law tends to lurch
from crisis to crisis and tends to exhibit the hallmarks of over-
reaction. Yet we must recognise that the preservation of order is
itself a reaction either to threats of or to actual disorder.

It is the function of the law and of the police to combat disorder
or threats of disorder. It is the function of the social reformer and
politician to prevent such threats of disorder arising in the first
place. Recently the then Chief Constable of Sussex, Sir George
Terry, speaking at the 1980 conference of the Association of
Chief Police Officers at Eastbourne, paraded three police officers
on stage to make this point. One officer was dressed as a Bow
Street runner, one as a conventionally attired policeman such as
we would be accustomed to meet every day in the street, the third
was dressed in para-military uniform bearing a striking resemblance to a member of the armed forces. His message was that so
long as society continues to become more violent, and as breakdowns in order become more serious, then the means of
preserving order must move forward. If the law is inadequate in
itself, then methods must change and as a last resort the police
must be equipped to enable them to preserve order. In the light of
these comments we move to a consideration of the law as it is
currently operated to combat violence and disorder as we
experience them today.

Violence and disorder have frequently been described as
'shocking' – see for example the comments of the Home

Secretary, Mr. Hurd, in the House of Commons in October 1985. Yet turmoil in society is by no means a new phenomenon, although it is true to say that many individual outbreaks of disorder and rioting have novel elements. The agencies and laws of enforcement and preserving the peace need to be responsive to these factors. The whole process of preservation of the peace is to some extent hampered by the sad fact that very many outbreaks of disorder have been associated with social grievances, not least of which have been industrial disputes and reactions to social deprivation.

There are several perspectives that can be adopted as to the nature of outbreaks of disorder. A liberal perspective sees disorder as a reaction to social conditions which may help to generate improvement. Viewed in this light mere suppression will not remedy the root causes and, if the tensions which create disorder are sufficiently great, suppression may well enhance the violence. A radical perspective goes further and suggests that violent disorder is a legitimate contribution to political debate. Here the objectives which are to be achieved will militate against containment and indeed may indicate that any attempt to suppress the disorder should be opposed with force. A third perspective is that violent disorder is purposeless and irrational and can thus be characterised simply as criminal. By focusing simply on disorder alone, the law tends to fall in with this last perspective. Lord Scarman in his inquiry into the Brixton Disorders seemed to accept that social causes may create an atmosphere where violence is likely or predictable, but that violent disorder itself cannot be excused. The law focuses on the latter aspect and ignores considerations of the former.

The police duty, the preservation of peace and order, is defined by the law, but the law does not define the police role. The law says nothing about individual discretionary decisions to be made by the police nor about the individual methods of policing or allocation of resources so long as they fall within parameters which the courts are willing, if asked, to find acceptable. The field of operation of police discretion is vast, the ultimate objective alone is defined. That objective moreover has to be achieved with resources and manpower which are inevitably limited not so much by disorder as by the many demands made on the police in today's complex society. In an area where discretion is so wide, and difficult choices as to tactics are made, it is by no means surprising to find the police allying themselves to perspectives which simply elide violence and disorder and criminality.

One further point needs to be indicated at this part of the discussion, namely that notions of 'rule of law', though of common currency, are variously interpreted and are capable of variable definition. One notion of rule of law stresses a freedom under the law to enjoy civil liberties including a freedom from violence and a freedom from oppression. Another notion is that of rule by law as opposed to rule by force or violence. From another perspective the rule of law supports the established order and justifies the assumption of extra powers to preserve order in the face of violent disorder. There is however a paradox in this last notion of rule of law. It opposes violence because it is a threat to the established order but at the same time legitimates force in order to preserve the established order. We have returned to our starting point, we have accepted a dualism in our attitude to violence in our midst. The difference between violence and legitimate violence is not an easy one to establish on paper, yet harder still to establish in the minds of those who are confronted by one or the other.

If we look to current trends in the operational policing of disorder and public violence we find that previous notions of public self-control are somewhat dated. The police can no longer rely on the goodwill of people who take to the public stage to enable control to be exercised on a mutual basis. The recent trend has been towards exercising operational control over situations where public order is threatened or has actually broken down. The focus has shifted from the criminality of those at the heart of disorder to preventative powers which can be utilised to counter disorder. The simple fact that there is a mass picket or a mass demonstration means that there is at best a serious threat to the public peace and that the freedom of individuals to go about their business is placed in jeopardy. It has thus become important to control the number of people who gather together in public in order to facilitate control. The 'control of numbers' policy changes the focus of operation from the specific crimes to the 'indirect' crime of participating in activities which the police, using their preventative powers, have deemed unconducive to preserving the peace.

In the recent miners' strike of 1984/5 the 'intercept' policy evolved to control the number of pickets and others who might otherwise be present at places where disorder was reasonably apprehended to occur. There is a numerical threshold beyond which a group simply cannot be policed unless they exercise self-control. Beyond that threshold notions of policing according to individual criminality are mere fictions. The policy of setting up road blocks to reduce the number of miners and others entering the Nottinghamshire coal field appears to have had considerable success; in the six months to September 1984 some 160,000 people were estimated to have been turned back. What actually occurred at each stop is not altogether clear, but at all events the court in *Moss* v *McLachlan* (1984)[54] accepted that a legal power existed for a police officer to turn back members of the public where he reasonably apprehended a breach of the peace.

In a judgement regrettably reported only in *The Times*, Mr. Justice Skinner defined the true nature of preventative powers in such a way that if the police formed an honest and reasonable view that there was a real risk of a breach of the peace in close proximity in both place and time (here approximately $1\frac{1}{2}$ miles or less than 5 minutes by car) 'then conditions existed for preventative action'. He added that the real possibility of a breach of the peace justified preventative action and that the imminence or immediacy of the threat determined what action was reasonable (here halting a convoy of presumed pickets). The judgement is one of unusual clarity in this area of law and certainly narrows the scope for preventative action to something less than it was assumed to have been. It would not appear to justify the setting up of a road block some 100 miles away from the apprehended breach of the peace.

Perhaps *Moss* v *McLachlan* can be read as drawing a distinction between preventative and pre-emptive policing? Although the legal powers used by the police here are usually brought within the banner heading of 'preventative' powers, in some instances, for example at the Dartford Tunnel in March 1984, they appear to have been used as 'pre-emptive' powers. The distinction is that preventative powers may be used to prevent a likely breach of the peace, pre-emptive powers prevent that likelihood arising. The case law suggests that police powers may only be used where likelihood has arisen (see for example *Kavanagh* v *Hisock*, 1974).[55] The statutory example where pre-emptive powers are given is the Public Order Act 1936, section 3(2) and (3) (the power to ban marches) and this section specifically operates where preventative powers are believed to be insufficient to prevent 'serious public disorder'. Perhaps every use of pre-emptive powers should be so limited. Preventative policing has a valid place in an ordered society, pre-emptive policing is rather one of the hallmarks of an oppressed society. At the very least the use of pre-emptive powers should be confined within well defined circumstances. That definition is a legitimate responsibility of the courts in the absence of statutory intervention.

If we return to the factor of numbers it will be recalled that, in practical terms, once a group of people exceeds a certain threshold size it cannot be contained within the bounds of order. That threshold may be very large if the members of the group exercise great self-control, but if such self-control is lacking then any group which exceeds the number which can be contained by the available police resources constitutes a threat to an ordered society. The mass picket of Saltley (1972) was perhaps the outstanding recent example of this, and perhaps the initial disorder at the outset of the St. Paul's riots was another. The 'intercept' policy used during the miners' strike is one example of an attempt to limit the size of groups gathering in public. There were others used by the police. They sought to limit pickets to those who were present at their own place of work. By reference to the Employment Act 1980, section 16 and to the Home Office Code on picketing, police sought to determine the bounds of picketing activities with regard to the criminal law according to rules set down by the civil law in relation to immunity from civil suit. The important point was that the police were seeking to prevent the build-up of a large mass of 'flying' pickets, i.e. to prevent the build-up of a group whose size and goals made containment by normal police methods most unlikely. The situation simply would not tolerate mere containment policing of all those who wished to be present.

Several other aspects of the policing of the miners' strike contributed to keeping down the number of people gathering together in public places. The vast number of arrests made when compared with the much lesser number of prosecutions seems to suggest that arrest was used not as a preliminary step in the process leading to charge and conviction but as a process in itself. By this means many people could be removed from the 'heart of the action' and perhaps some weaker souls might be deterred from joining the group causing disorder. The same can be said of the frequent use of bind-overs. If someone is bound over on conditions by magistrates then he faces severe penalties if he joins a group which is threatening disorder or which has caused a breakdown in order. Much controversy surrounded the conditions attached by magistrates to remands on bail. The controversy centred on two aspects: the one the readiness of magistrates to agree to what rapidly became standard form conditions; the other the sweeping nature of the conditions, in particular that an individual be restricted to his own place of work. The policy of sweeping bail restrictions was approved by Lord Chief Justice Lane in *R* v *Mansfield Justices ex. p. Sharkey* (1985).[56] The original purpose of attaching conditions to bail, namely to prevent further offences, seems to have been broadened to encompass elements of control as well, though the court did refer in that case to the real, not fanciful, risk of further offences. Thus practical considerations determined that the margins of legal powers were explored to reduce numbers to a manageable proportion.

The police practice during the miners' strike also relied heavily on sufficient police being available in circumstances of disorder. In recent years the training of police officers from all forces in public order policing has both been standardised and improved. Each force has an obligation to provide mutual aid to any other force requiring assistance. Each force maintains police support units, each consisting of trained groups which are highly mobile. The whole in times of crisis is closely supervised by the National Reporting Centre headed by the current president of the Association of Chief Police Officers. The ready availability of vast numbers of riot-trained officers enables the police to control and thus contain larger groups and less large groups which are for one reason or another unwilling to exercise self-control. The important point to realise is that the law can itself only operate in a more or less ordered environment. It cannot simply operate regardless of the circumstances. Any appreciation of the contribution which the law can make to the resolution of violent disorder in society must recognise that if disorder or rather the breakdown of order reaches a certain threshold then appeals to the law and agencies of the law are likely to be disappointed. We have seen how the orthodox criminal law has limited utility where the breakdown of order is great. For this reason wide, even sweeping, preventative powers are available to the police and others to enable them to preserve that sufficiently ordered state of society which is a prerequisite for the operation of the criminal law. The development and structuring of police resources enables the law to be utilised in disordered and difficult circumstances. But nonetheless there are limits to what can be achieved. If order degenerates to such a degree that there is a violent breakdown in our social order then it is somewhat naive to look to public order laws, both substantive and preventative, to redress the situation. The problem is not one of law but one of order and the ordering of society is a job for the politician, not the judge or the policeman.

When the situation degenerates 'in extremis' it is of paramount importance that order is restored. That is justified not by appeals to law but by reference to the necessity for an ordered state. The situation is almost one of no law. The classic example is of course the operation of the old Riot Act, 1714.[57] If twelve or more people 'riotously and tumultuously' gathered together to the 'disturbance of the publick peace' and remained together for over an hour after the reading of the proclamation by the magistrates then deadly force could be used, frequently by the military, to disperse them. Section 3 of the Act expressly indemnified those engaged in suppressing the riot should any of the rioters be killed or injured. The process was designed to provide a means for the speedy re-establishment of order. It bears a striking resemblance to some aspects of the policing of the miners' strike, in particular to the events at Orgreave. The equipment, organisation and tactics of the police appeared designed to forcefully re-establish a climate of order rather than simply to enforce the criminal laws or to utilise orthodox laws of prevention. There were remarkably few arrests at Orgreave. There are obvious dangers in this approach. It must not be forgotten that the Riot Act procedures were to be used as a matter of last resort. There were procedural safeguards, the reading of the proclamation and the hour to disperse. It would be a matter of the utmost concern if modern parallels of the forceful re-establishment of order were to be used any more readily than their predecessors.

It is thus a matter of prime importance that situations where the need to re-establish sufficient order to enable the law to operate should arise as infrequently as humanly possible. To achieve this we must not look to the law but must look elsewhere. The law facilitates the resolution of disorder but cannot resolve large scale breakdowns in our ordered society such as we have experienced of late.

## CONCLUSION

In such a brief study it is unwise to come to any dogmatic conclusions, but those who are either concerned about the law or about reform of the law insofar as it touches upon violence and public disorder should perhaps understand the difficulties under which the law labours. Violence tends to be a group activity, but the law punishes individual acts which break the criminal code. To punish one person for another's wrongful act would be an infringement of important civil freedoms even though they both may fall within a group which as a group had committed criminal acts. The definition of public order crimes is an elusive task. The law needs to be at the same time clear and yet workable and effective. If it is not, then there is a real risk that resort to the law may exacerbate the disorder. Most of all the law must be seen not as words on a page, but as the body of tools which human actors use in frequently tense, but essentially human situations. This is of vital importance when discretionary powers are in issue. The tendency to overreact or to get emotionally involved in what one is doing is an ever present factor. The vast powers of prevention must be utilised to preserve order and not to create oppression. This involves judgement about what constitutes an ordered society and whether or not individual instances of disorder are sufficient to take the actors involved out of the realms of an ordered society.

But nonetheless the law has limits which no amount of tinkering with definitions or powers can transcend. Rule of law is a characteristic of an ordered society. Any society needs a certain degree of order before the agencies of the law can function. That is a prerequisite. When the breakdown of order creates an environment where the law cannot function, where people are hell-bent on breaking the law or where objectives can only be achieved by disregarding the law then the problem is not one of law reform. The vital need is to secure again an ordered society in which we can live according to the rule of law and where violence does not supplant other means of attaining social goals. That function is the job of the political reformer. It is only as an adjunct to that process that we should turn to reform of the law.

## NOTES

1. Chapter 3.
2. Report on the Red Lion Square Disorders of 15th June 1974 (Cmnd 5919, 1975).
3. Brownlie, *Law of Public Order and National Security* (ed. Supperstone, 2nd ed., 1981) ch. 1.
4. See Smith and Hogan, *The Criminal Law* (5th ed., 1983), ch. 12.
5. [1970] 1 W.L.R. 562.
6. 20 Feb. 1980.
7. [1970] Crim. L.R. 553.
8. See eg. Home Office Working Party Report on Vagrancy and Street Offences (1976).
9. *The Times*, 29 Nov. 1985.
10. D.G.T. Williams, *Keeping the Peace* (1967).
11. Preliminary Report (1984) para. 1: 8.
11a. [1935] 2 K.B. 249.
12. Detailed analysis of these crimes can be found in Brownlie (op. cit.) and S. Bailey, D. Harris, B. Jones, *Civil Liberties Cases and Materials* (2nd ed., 1985).
13. See Bailey, Harris, Jones (op. cit.), ch. 3, p. 3.
14. [1982] Q.B. 416.
15. [1982] A.C. 540.
16. [1973] A.C. 854.
17. [1976] Crim. L.R. 451.
18. [1982] Crim. L.R. 827.
19. [1982] 3 W.L.R. 523.

20. Cmnd 8092, 1981.
21. An interesting insight into reasonable suspicion can be gained from D. Powis, *The Signs of Crime* (1977).
22. Cmnd 8427, 1981.
23. [1974] Cr. App. Rep. 120.
24. [1974] A.C. 104.
25. (1882) 9 Q.B.D. 308.
26. [1902] 1 K.B. 167.
27. [1970] Crm. L.R. 656, see generally Brownlie (op. cit.), ch. 6, p.6.
28. (1970) *The Times*, 10 Feb.
29. (1977) *The Times*, 10 May.
30. See Bailey, Harris, Jones (op. cit.), ch. 3, p. 162.
31. See M. Kettle and L. Hodges, *Uprising* (1982).
32. [1966] A.C. 591.
33. [1973] A.C. 964, see Brownlie (op. cit.), ch. 7.
34. [1976] Crim. L.R. 693.
35. Op. cit.
36. See generally Williams (op. cit.), ch. 4.
37. Cmnd 5919, 1975.
38. [1982] Q.B. 458.
39. See note 27 above.
40. See Brownlie (op. cit), pp. 105 ff.
41. (1980) Cr. App. Rep. 221.
42. See Ld. Scarman, Cmnd 5919, 1975.
43. (1864) 17 I.C.L.R. 1, see Bailey, Harris, Jones (op. cit.), pp. 172 ff.
44. (1883) Cox C.C. 435.
45. [1936] 1 K.B. 218.
46. [1960] 3 All E.R. 660.
47. See note 15 above.
48. See note 46.
49. See note 45 above.
50. See Brownlie (op. cit.), ch. 14.
51. See Williams (op. cit.), ch. 4.
52. Report No. 123, *Criminal Law: Offences relating to Public Order* (1983).
53. Bill 129 of 1985/6.
54. *The Times*, 29 Nov. 1984.
55. [1974] Q.B. 600.
56. [1985] 1 All E.R. 193.
57. For a useful account see Williams (op. cit.), ch. 1.

# CHAPTER SIX

# PATHWAYS OUT OF TERRORISM FOR DEMOCRATIC SOCIETIES

## Paul Wilkinson

Terrorism is not a synonym for violence and insurgency in general. It is a special kind of violence, a weapons system that can be used on its own or as part of a whole repertoire of unconventional warfare. In Central America, for example, terrorism is typically used in conjunction with rural guerrilla warfare and with economic and political warfare in all-out bids to topple government. But in Western Europe, which experiences about 40 per cent of all international terrorist incidents annually, terrorism is usually unaccompanied by any wider insurgency. It is extreme, often indiscriminate violence directed at innocent people, but it is at the pre-insurgency phase.

Terrorism can be briefly defined as coercive intimidation, or more fully as the systematic use of murder, injury, and destruction, or threat of same, to create a climate of terror, to publicise a cause, and to coerce a wider target into submitting to the terrorist's aims. International terrorism is terrorism exported across international frontiers or used against foreign targets in the terrorists' country of origin. There is no case of purely domestic terrorism, but there are, of course, many campaigns in which the political violence is concentrated in a single national territory or region (e.g. the Irish Republican Army and the Basque and Corsican terrorists).

A major characteristic of political terror is its indiscriminate nature. This is not to deny that terrorists generally have a specific human 'target', whether individual or collective, which they intend shall be the victim of the most direct physical harm. Quite apart from the physical danger to persons who are not preselected targets, there is the unavoidable side-effect of wide-spread fear that others might be harmed. As Raymond Aron remarks in one of his most percipient observations on terror:

> An action of violence is labelled 'terrorist' when its psychological effects are out of proportion to its purely physical result. In this sense, the so-called indiscriminate acts of revolutionaries are terrorist, as were the Anglo-American zone bombings. The lack of discrimination helps to spread fear, for if no one in particular is a target, no one can be safe.[1]

Terrorists are frequently prepared to engage in the indiscriminate murder of civilians. All men, women, and children, regardless of their role or position in society, may be regarded as potential victims for the sake of the 'cause'. As a policy the waging of terror necessarily involves disregarding the rules and conventions of war: non-combatants, hostages, prisoners-of-war, and neutrals have no inviolable rights in their eyes.

It is also characteristic of acts of terror that they appear entirely unpredictable and arbitrary to the society which suffers them. One writer has expressed this point very clearly: 'no observance of commands, no matter how punctilious, on the part of the prospective victims can ensure their safety'.[2] There are of course many instances of the individual victims of terroristic assassination or mass murder being given preliminary warning that they are to die. The point is that such acts are only 'selective' and 'predictable' according to the rationalisations of the terrorists. As Malraux writes, 'le terroriste décidât seul exécutât seul',[3] and it is in this sense true to describe terrorism as a peculiar kind of tyranny in which the potential victim is unable to do anything to avoid his destruction because the terrorist is operating and judging on the basis of his own idiosyncratic code of norms and values. Do these characteristics of unpredictability and arbitrariness also apply in the case of the repressive terror of the state? There are two major reasons why they are common also to state terror. First, leaders and agencies of force in the state, who have acquired the preponderance of coercive power, may disregard the underlying values and norms of the existing law with impunity within their domain. Second, tyrannical dictators or totalitarian governments tend in the process of consolidating their power to subvert and manipulate the legal structure in order to forge it into a weapon of oppression of their internal opponents. Under such conditions, instead of the sovereignty of the state and the rule of law being used solely to apply punishment for clearly defined crimes or offences, judicial acts may become what Hobbes termed acts of hostility. For Hobbes a hostile act 'falls not under the name of Punishment'[4] because it is an act against one who is not politically obedient to the legal authority (i.e. the state). Punishment, argues Hobbes, is reserved for those citizens of a state who have broken the law. It is 'an Evil inflicted by publique authority . . . to the end that the will of men may thereby better be disposed to obedience'.[5] But in response to an act of hostility, he claimed 'all infliction of evil is lawful',[6] that is, there are no limits to the violence that can be committed. It is clear that many tyrannies and terrorisms have sought to confuse this important distinction by lending their actions a quasi-legal rationale. They resort to defining any action they choose as an act of political disobedience, thus claiming that by their hostile acts they are in reality punishing political crimes.

Political terror can also be differentiated from other forms of violence, agitation, intimidation and coercion by virtue of its extreme and ruthlessly destructive methods. These may range from genocide, massacre and political murder and torture at one end of the scale of violence, to physical beatings, harassment and defamation campaigns at the other. For any large-scale campaign of repressive or of revolutionary terror, the terrorists find it necessary to arm themselves adequately to check any possible resistance. Whereas spears and machetes were once adequate weapons in African tribal regimes of terror, and the famous sect of the Assassins in the eleventh and twelfth centuries used the dagger, modern terrorists must depend upon a minimal supply of guns and explosives. The factor of dependence upon weaponry, combined with the reliance of many terrorist movements and agencies upon a military organisational structure and style, underlines the close relationship between terrorism and war. Indeed, many American and French scholars have been so impressed by this affinity that they have tended to study terror exclusively in the context of 'internal war' and problems of 'counter-insurgency'.

It is in practice extremely difficult to draw clear boundaries between war and terror. E.V. Walter, in his pioneering sociological analysis of the regime of terror, argues that, unlike civil terror, military terror aims ultimately at exterminating the enemy. Civil terror, he asserts, is always an instrument of power aimed at the control and not destruction of the population: 'When violence is employed in the service of power, the limit of force is the destruction of the thing that is forced'.[7] But there are two serious confusions in Walter's argument. First, we cannot assume that all wars are wars of extermination: even in modern wars distinctions are sometimes made between the civilian population and the armed forces of protagonists, and one of the normal strategic objectives is still the acquisition and control of enemy territories and their inhabitants. Second, and more important, internal revolutionary and state terror can both be directed at the deliberate destruction of whole social groups who have been designated as enemies. Terrorists may believe such a policy of liquidation to be necessary in order to capture or sustain their political control, or it may be dictated by ideological reasons, or it may derive from motives of hatred, vengeance or even sadism or mass hysteria, or a combination of these factors. The point to be made is that, historically, acts of civil terror have not, unfortunately, always stopped short at the subjugation of certain real or imagined opponents. Totalitarian regimes of terror have committed crimes against humanity on a vast scale. We have no right to assume that the perpetrators of civil terror will arrive by some rational calculation at a notional limit to violence, and that they will always rule out extermination. As for the implications for political control, mass murders will intensify rather than extinguish the general terror: everyone in the population will be terrified lest they be caught in the next wave of terror. Thus, although this paper does not attempt a detailed analysis of war terror (i.e. terroristic usages in military conflict), our discussion must necessarily include consideration of the many kinds of destruction against the civil population which can be understood as what Hobbes called 'hostile acts', or acts of war against the population.

What fundamentally distinguishes terrorism from other forms of organised violence is not simply its severity, but its features of amorality and antinomianism. Terrorists either profess indifference to existing moral codes or else claim exemption from all such obligations. Political terror, if it is waged consciously and deliberately, is implicitly prepared to sacrifice all moral and humanitarian considerations for the sake of some political end. Ideologies of terrorism assume that the death and suffering of those who are innocent of any crime are means entirely justified by their political ends. In their most explicit and candidly amoral form such terrorist rationalisations amount to a Nietzschean doctrine of the Will to Power. Might is right; terror can always be justified as the expediency of the strong; and such Judaeo-Christian notions as mercy, compassion and conscience must go with the weak to the wall of history. Political terror is not always justified in such explicit terms. Some utopian or messianic sects and movements that have resorted to terror have attempted a teleological justification, generally involving the rejection of all existing ethical principles and codes on the grounds that morality is manipulated in the interests of the rulers. In some cases it is argued that the acts of terror are necessary sacrifices to be made on the journey towards introducing a new revolutionary order which will introduce a New Man and a New Order and, of course, a Revolutionary Morality. But, of course, the first task is that the existing order and morality are destroyed.

We have thus identified some of the key characteristics common to all forms of political terror: indiscriminateness, unpredictability, arbitrariness, ruthless destructiveness and the implicitly amoral and antinomian nature of a terrorist's challenge. There remains the important distinction between political terror and political terrorism. Clearly political terror may occur in isolated acts and also in the form of extreme, indiscriminate and arbitrary mass violence, the kind of insurrectionary outburst that characterised the lynchings and sackings at the height of the popular terror in parts of revolutionary France. Such terror is not systematic, it is unorganised and is often impossible to control. 'Therefore neither one isolated act, nor a series of random acts is terrorism'.[8] Political terrorism, properly speaking, is a sustained policy involving the waging of organised terror either on the part of the state, a movement or faction, or by a small group of individuals. Systematic terrorism invariably entails some organisational structure, however rudimentary, and some kind of theory or ideology of terror.

## CAN THE END JUSTIFY THE MEANS?

Much confusion occurs in the debate on the morality of terrorism because of a failure to distinguish between ends and means. Terrorism is a *method* which can be used for an infinite variety of goals. The cliché that one man's terrorist is another man's freedom fighter simply reflects the paradox that many groups use terror in pursuit of a cause that most liberal democrats in principle regard as just, the goal of self-determination or national liberation.

Yet even in cases where we have firm grounds for believing that a group has a legitimate grievance or sense of grave injustice, this does not mean that we should refrain from posing the question 'Does a just cause justify the use of terrorism by its supporters?' Terrorism is inherently and inevitably a means of struggle involving indiscriminate and arbitrary violence against the innocent. It is almost universally agreed among the citizens of liberal democracies that the method of terrorism is morally indefensible in a free society in which, by definition, there are always other ways of campaigning for a cause, methods which do not involve a fundamental attack on the human rights of fellow citizens.

The writer takes an even more determined moral position against the use of terrorism, whether by states or factions. It is frequently claimed by the terrorists that actions such as bombings, hostage-taking, and assassinations are the only means they have for removing a tyrannical or oppressive authoritarian regime. This claim does not bear serious examination. There are *always* some other means, including moral resistance and civil disobedience and well-planned and concerted economic and political action, which either alone or in combination may prove extremely effective in removing an unpleasant regime with the minimum of violence. There is no case of terrorism removing an autocracy, but there are many inspiring examples of the relatively bloodless removal of dictatorships, including Portugal and Spain in the mid-1970s, and Haiti and the Philippines in early 1986.

Thus, I would argue, we should question the received wisdom of the radical left which constantly asserts that terrorism is permissible, even desirable, as a weapon against non-democratic systems. From the humanitarian point of view there is a stench of double standards about such a policy. Should we be less concerned about the rights of the innocent in non-democratic societies? What right have we, sitting in the comfort of our free political systems, to condone a method of 'freedom fighting' which robs innocent civilians of life, maims many others, and destroys their property? And how can we ignore the historical evidence that those who use such methods become corrupted and criminalised by the savagery of the infliction of terrorism? Moreover, the idea that terrorism is a precise, highly controlled, almost surgical, strategy is a cruel illusion. Once a society becomes launched on a spiral of terror and counter-terror, there may be no way of stopping the carnage. Terrorism will become interwoven with the criminal sub-culture: for many it will become a way of life. The violence of the Internal Macedonian Revolutionary Organisation (IMRO) in the Balkans in the early twentieth century, and parts of Latin America and the Lebanon today, are gruesome examples of the corrupting effects of habitual terrorism.

### AN ALTERNATIVE TO WAR? OR A THREAT TO PEACE?

There can be no doubt that terrorism, despite its savage inhumanity to civilians, is a lesser evil than modern war. Even in a relatively short-lived civil war in a small country the level of violence will be vastly more lethal and destructive. For example, more people died in the Lebanese civil war, 1974-76, than were killed in the entire decade of international terrorism 1975-85.

Terrorism is sometimes described as a form of 'surrogate warfare'. In the sense that it is often adopted as a low-cost/low-risk/potentially high yield instrument of foreign policy by pro-terrorist states, this is a useful concept. But it would be a dangerous error to assume that it therefore follows that the international community can face the growth of terrorism with equanimity. For just as severe internal terrorism often leads to a full-scale bloody civil war, so international terrorism has sometimes triggered international war, with all its accompanying wider dangers to international peace. Let us not forget that it was the assassination at Sarajevo in 1914 which was the catalyst for the First World War. More recently, the attempt on the life of Ambassador Argov in 1982 helped to spark the Israeli invasion of Lebanon, with all its inevitable dangers of escalation to a general war in the Middle East.

Democracies are clearly vulnerable to terrorist attacks because of the openness of their societies and the ease of movement across and within frontiers. It is always easy for extremists to exploit democratic freedoms with the aim of destroying democracy. But a well-established democratic political system also has enormous inner strengths. By definition, the majority of the population see the government as legitimate and accountable. They willingly cooperate in the upholding of the law, and they rally to defend democracy against the petty tyrants who try to substitute the gun and the bomb for the ballot box. There is no case in the modern history of terrorism in which a European democracy has been destroyed by a terrorist group and replaced by a pro-terrorist regime.

Even so, it is clear that prolonged and intensive terrorism can be very damaging to the democratic governments and societies that experience it. For example, in Northern Ireland and Spain, terrorism not only fundamentally attacks innocent life and rights, it aims to undermine the democratic values, institutions, processes, and rule of law. By scaring away investment and disrupting industry and commerce, terrorism can gravely weaken the economy. At its most intensive, terrorist violence serves to incite hatred, promote and provoke inter-communal conflict and violence, and destroy the middle ground of normal politics. If unchecked, terrorism can easily escalate to a civil war situation, which the terrorist may seek to exploit in order to establish a terrorist-style dictatorship.

In the long run, the threat to human freedom from the spread of terrorism in Third World areas is far more serious. For terrorism in these often highly unstable areas is much more likely to lead to the undermining of fragile democratic governments and is widely used as part of the repertoire of revolutionary movements to bring about Marxist takeovers of Third World states. These wider revolutionary conflicts clearly alter the regional balance of power in Third World areas. They also threaten general economic interests, such as access to oil and raw materials, and this threatens general lines of maritime communication at strategic chokepoints.

Internationally, terrorism is far more than a challenge to the rule of law and a clear threat to individual life and safety. It has the potential to become far more than a minor problem of law and order. For the United States, the major target of international terrorism all over the world, terrorism can be a major national security problem. For example, the handling of the seizure of the entire United States diplomatic mission in Tehran in 1979 became a colossal burden to the Carter Administration, crippling other activities and weakening U.S. morale and prestige internationally, particularly in the Middle East. More recently, the tragic bombings of U.S. marines in Lebanon not only took large numbers of lives, but also severely curtailed President Reagan's military options in the Middle East and made it impossible for him to maintain a U.S. presence in Lebanon, either through the multinational force or independently. The suicide bombers' atrocity reached U.S. opinion, Congress, and the media, as it was clearly designed to do.

## WHY HAS THE COLLECTIVE RESPONSE OF THE DEMOCRACIES BEEN SO INEFFECTIVE?

In a world of sovereign states, it is inherently difficult to secure effective international cooperation. Despite the fact that Western states cooperate in such organisations as the OECD and NATO, it is extremely hard for them to cooperate in the sensitive area of internal security and law and order. On such matters, they have traditionally taken the view that the national government has total sovereign control. Western politicians and judiciaries are as chauvinistic in this respect as other states, despite the many moral and legal values they have in common with fellow Western governments.

A major political difficulty in cooperation against terrorism is the lack of a clear single forum for Western democratic cooperation. The European Community does not include all the major Western states, and in any case it is primarily concerned with economic matters. NATO, though it has a larger membership, is by no means comprehensive and essentially remains an intergovernmental organisation in which member states jealously guard their national sovereignty. It has been left to the Council of Europe to mount the most serious effort at West European legal cooperation against terrorism, the European Convention for the Suppression of Terrorism, but the Council lacks political weight and influence and its convention remains unratified by key states such as France and is unenforceable.

Some Western democracies have little or no direct experience of terrorism, and thus cannot see the importance of the problem. Enthusiasm for action often dissipates rapidly once shock at a specific outrage has died away. Some Western governments are unwilling to sacrifice or endanger commercial outlets, possible markets, trade links, or sources of oil or raw materials by taking really tough action against pro-terrorist states like Libya. Some states are also afraid of attracting revenge attacks from terrorist states; they hope to buy security by appeasement. Some have a double standard; they insist on regarding some terrorists as 'freedom fighters' who need not be condemned (e.g. Irish-American attitudes to IRA, French attitude to Armenian terrorists, Greek attitude to the Palestine Liberation Organisation).

Worst of all is the widespread defeatist illusion, assiduously cultivated by the propaganda of the terrorist movements, that democracies can do nothing to defeat terrorism. This is dangerous rubbish; look at the success of countries like Canada, against the FLQ, and Italy against the Red Brigades. We do have experience and knowledge showing us how to defeat even severe campaigns of terrorism. It is basically up to each democratic government to learn and apply these lessons, and to improve its cooperation with fellow democracies.

### PATHWAYS OUT OF TERRORISM

The experience of modern terrorism in democratic societies has shown that there are no simple solutions. There are many pathways out of terrorism: some lead in opposite directions, while others provide alternative routes to strengthening democracy and reducing violence. Let us briefly identify six main possible pathways out of terrorism:

(i) the terrorists solve the problem on *their* terms: they achieve their goals and abandon the violence as it is no longer seen as necessary. This has only happened very rarely. In a number of colonial independence struggles in the 1950s and 1960s (Palestine, Algeria, Cyprus, Aden) something very close to this did occur. But the conditions of decaying colonialism provided exceptional opportunities for terrorists which no longer exist in the 1980s: for example, the colonial regimes lacked the will to maintain their control and were gravely economically and militarily weakened by the exertions of World War II. The terrorists in most cases had vast popular support from their own populations.

(ii) The terrorists perceive the inevitable failure of their campaign, or in any case grow weary of it, and give up their violent struggle without having achieved their goals. An example of this was the abandonment of the struggle by the IRA in Northern Ireland in 1962.

(iii) The terrorist campaign may be eradicated within the borders of the state by determined and efficient military action. For example, a draconian military campaign virtually wiped out the Tupamaros campaign in Uruguay. But this was at the heavy cost of the virtual suspension of democratic government in Uruguay and its replacement by military rule. A frequent effect of this strategy is to drive the terrorist residue into exile. The campaign may thus be continued abroad, including attacks on the diplomats of the target state, with the terrorist hope of carrying their fight back to their homeland.

(iv) A fourth scenario is a political solution on the state's terms which nevertheless makes sufficient concessions to genuine and deeply felt grievances of a particular group that in effect it dries up the water in which the terrorist 'fish' swim. There have been a few examples of remarkably successful use of this strategy. It was extremely effective in the case of the South Tirol (Alto Adige) where the autonomy measure passed by the Italian Senate in 1971 defused a violent campaign. But in most cases this method has only limited success because there are always 'maximalists' or 'irreconcilables' among the terrorists who refuse to abandon the struggle unless or until their absolute demands are met. Hence, despite the bold and imaginative measures taken by the French and Spanish governments respectively to introduce a real regional autonomy in Corsica and the Basque region, hard-line terrorist groups in each case have continued to wage violence.

(v) Many democratic states attempt to deal with internal terrorism as essentially a problem of law enforcement and judicial control, viewing terrorist actions as serious crimes and dealing with them firmly under the criminal code. There have been some remarkably successful applications of this approach, for example against the early generations of the Red Army Faction in West Germany and against the Red Brigades and other terrorist groups in Italy. In both these cases it is true that the laws and the judicial process had to be strengthened in order to cope with the ruthlessness and cunning of the terrorists. But it is manifestly the case that in both countries essential democratic values and institutions and the rule of law remain intact despite these long and bitter campaigns of terrorists to undermine the state and to provoke it into over-reaction

There are often serious residual problems with this approach, however. Some terrorists will inevitably succeed in escaping justice by fleeing abroad, as has been the case with many Red Brigades and Red Army Faction members who have fled to France, 'Terre d'Asile'. From their new bases abroad they may then continue to wage violence and attempt to rebuild their networks within their home countries. Nor does the problem end when terrorists are successfully apprehended, tried and con- victed. As our penal systems are ill-adapted and under-equipped to handle large numbers of imprisoned terrorists, it is all too easy for militant and determined terrorists, with considerable ex- perience of covert activity outside gaol, to begin to re-establish their terrorist organisations within the prison system. In addition, using the aid of pro-terrorist lawyers and friends, they can even hope to establish a network outside prison which they can direct, or at least strongly influence, from inside gaol. Hence the law enforcement solution by itself is inevitably incomplete. Without additional measures there is the strong likelihood of new terrorist movements recreating themselves from the ashes of the old.

(vi) Finally there is the educative solution, in which the combination of educational effort by democratic political parties, the mass media, trade unions, churches, schools, colleges, and other major social institutions, succeeds in persuading the terrorists, or a sufficient proportion of their supporters, that terrorism is both undesirable and counter-productive to the realisation of the terrorists' political ideals. This approach is, of course, fraught with enormous difficulties and requires many years of patient work before it yields results. It has rarely been tried on a major scale. However, small-scale experiments in the re-education and rehabilitation of former members of ETA-militar and the Red Brigades indicate that it can be extraordinarily successful in certain cases.

Democratic pathways out of terrorism (iv), (v) and (vi) are obviously not mutually exclusive. Undoubtedly the most effective policy will be multi-pronged, involving skilfully coordinated elements of each. However, with the exception of models (i) and (ii), in which the terrorist group itself takes the decision to abandon its violence, there is no sound basis for assuming that the *total* eradication of terrorist violence from democratic society is feasible. It is part of the price we must pay for our democratic freedoms that some may choose to abuse these freedoms for the purposes of destroying democracy, or some other goal.

It follows that an essential part of democratic efforts must be to provide effective pathways out of terrorism for the individual. By so doing we will constantly be aiming to minimise the threat of residual or irreconcilable terrorism which may otherwise slowly regroup and regain sufficient support and strength to launch fresh campaigns of violence. In this constant moral and psychological battle of attrition, democratic authorities must constantly seek more imaginative and effective ways of enabling individual members of terrorist organisations to make a complete break with their comrades and leaders who, for their part, strive to keep their members under an iron grip.

### INDIVIDUAL PATHWAYS OUT OF TERRORISM

The first thing to understand about the problem is the colossal pressure which keeps the individual terrorist bonded to the terrorist group. He or she will have been intensively indoctrinated, actually brainwashed, into seeing the world through terrorist spectacles. They will have been taught to hate everyone associated with government and the legal system, especially the police, with a blind loathing. They will be schooled into suspecting the authorities' every move, habitually disbelieving their every statement, constantly vigilant for new traps or ruses set by the 'enemy'. Moreover, they will have it instilled into them that the only important thing in life is the furtherance of their cause. Every involvement in a terrorist action will further reinforce this and will be rationalised as the dedicated pursuit of justice. They are taught to see every bombing, each shooting, each fresh act of violence against the 'enemy' state, as a heroic act, as the living of the true revolutionary existence. Terrorist violence is thus transvalued in their minds to provide meaning and purpose to their hitherto 'wasted' lives. Once this process of indoctrination and mental bonding to the ideology of the group has reached a certain point it is extremely difficult to bring the terrorists even to *question* their fundamental ideological assumptions and beliefs, let alone abandon them.

A second major constraint is the individual terrorist's fear of his/her own group. Terror has always been the method used to ruthlessly control discipline within the conspiratorial world of the terrorist organisation. Kneecapping, shooting in the hand or foot, and torture, are punishments frequently meted out for relatively minor violations of the rules laid down by the leadership. Major infractions or repeated disobedience of the leaders' orders usually mean death. If the individual terrorist is tempted to 'disappear' or is suspected of having gone over to the side of the authorities, the terrorists will try to mete out vengeance on their closest family members. Faced with such deadly threats from their own group, it is little wonder that few of them find the courage to try to break with the past.

Third, even if they can break these bonds, some individual terrorists will be deterred from breaking with their group because of the apparently insuperable difficulties of rehabilitating themselves in normal society. They will be in constant fear of being handed over to the authorities. In order to get a job, buy a car, or obtain a home, they will need false identity papers, and will be in constant fear of their true identity being discovered by their employers and by the police. If they wish to get married, register a birth or death, obtain a passport, open a bank account or acquire social security benefits, then these difficulties will be compounded. If the terrorist knows that the normal sentence for the crime/s of which they have been guilty is severe, say at least ten years' imprisonment, they may calculate that the dangers of leaving the group's protective 'underground' cover and the added risk of arrest outweigh the disadvantages of continued terrorist membership.

Countries such as Italy and the United Kingdom already have some considerable experience of the ways in which these conflicting pressures tug at the emotions and divide the loyalties of those who are hesitating on the brink of turning state's evidence. The 'repentant terrorist' legislation in Italy (which has now been permitted to lapse) and the 'supergrass' system in Northern Ireland, have both provided invaluable intelligence about the operations, membership and plans of their respective terrorist groups. It is notoriously difficult for the police to infiltrate the cell structures of modern terrorist organisations. Hence this type of 'inside information' from informers is often the sole means of securing the information to bring terrorists to trial and to convict them. This experience has also led to an intensification of the terrorist leaderships' attempts to punish and deter those who may seek to betray them, for they know that once such a process gets well under way it can rapidly demoralise and destroy their whole campaign. This underlines the absolute necessity of providing 'supergrasses' with new identities and secure new lives to protect them from assassination by their former comrades. In spite of this important and fascinating experience, which incidentally has hardly begun to be subjected to any serious research by social scientists, it must be said that our democratic legal and penal systems remain extraordinarily ill-fitted to the specialised tasks of winning over individual members of the terror organisations and setting about their long-term rehabilitation in normal society.

There are many who would deny the need to bother with such efforts. It is easy to pour cold water on theories and policies of rehabilitation which have proved of very limited value in application to conventional crime. Yet there is reason to believe that the terrorist who has been subjected to intensive political indoctrination and conditioned by the terrorist training and way of life is potentially susceptible to determined, skilful and well-planned re-education and rehabilitation techniques, if only we could make these available within our penal systems.

It is of course a very important consideration in any rule of law system that there should be no special privileges or discrimination in favour of those who plead political motives for their crimes of violence. According terrorists special status only serves to legitimise and perpetuate their own self-perception as 'freedom fighters' and 'heroes', and simultaneously undermines the general public's confidence in the impartiality and consistency of the judicial system. But why should we not be more innovative and sophisticated in our *application* of penal policy? The prisons already have the broad tasks of education and rehabilitation, though few have the resources to do these jobs well. There is already considerable flexibility in reviewing sentences and in the parole system. There is no reason whatever, in principle, why we should not make a more serious effort within the prisons to re-educate and rehabilitate, and to inject the expertise and relatively modest resources necessary to cope with the special problems of terrorist offenders, in just the same way that we make special provision for trying to wean drug addicts away from their addictions. In the long term such measures would make a substantial contribution by significantly reducing the danger of terrorist cells reconstituting within the prison systems and of terrorists returning to their careers of violence when ultimately released. Currently in most penal systems little or nothing is being done to open up these individual pathways out of terrorism. Intense efforts in this field will be required if they are to have any effect, and we should be under no illusion that it will be easy to win back the committed terrorist.

*          *          *

All these major elements of an effective policy to deal with terrorism ultimately depend on the moral strength and political will of democratic society. The best general defence of a democracy against the alienation and violence of extremism is the sensitivity and effectiveness of the system of government in attending to the basic needs of the people. In a famous passage in *Vivian Grey* that brilliant British statesman, Disraeli, reminds us

> that all power is a trust – that we are accountable for its exercise – that, from the people, and for the people, all springs, and all must exist.[9]

A democratic government that loses touch with this central principle risks not only losing the trust of its citizens, but ultimately its legitimacy. And it is only when there is a genuine crisis of democratic legitimacy that extremists have a chance of seizing power.[10]

## NOTES

Some parts of this essay were presented in a paper to the Commonwealth Law Conference, Jamaica, 1986

1. Raymond Aron, *Peace and War* (London, 1966), p. 170.
2. S. Andreski, 'Terror' in Julius Gould and William L. Kolb (eds.), *A Dictionary of the Social Sciences* (Glencoe, 1964).
3. André Malraux, *La Condition Humaine* (Paris, 1946), p. 189.
4. Thomas Hobbes, *Leviathan* (London, OUP edition 1947), p. 241.
5. Ibid, p. 238.
6. Ibid, p. 241.
7. Eugene V. Walter, *Terror and Resistance* (New York, 1969), p. 14.
8. Martha Crenshaw Hutchison, 'The Concept of Revolutionary Terrorism', *The Journal of Conflict Resolution*, 16, 3 (Sept. 1972).
9. *Vivian Grey*, bk vi, ch. 7.
10. For a full analysis of the implications of terrorism for liberal democracy and the problems of response see the author's *Terrorism and the Liberal State*, 2nd edition (London, Macmillan 1986).

# CHAPTER SEVEN

# IS THERE A MEANINGFUL RESPONSE?

## Marcus Braybrooke

The complexity and intractability of the violence in our society and world, which other authors have indicated, could easily discourage any attempt to combat it. Indeed despair and cynicism themselves help to engender violence, and this is part of the terrorist's intention. When for fear of possible violence people cease to take part in legitimate activities, such as travelling abroad, they concede victory to the men of violence.

In every religion there is the hope that the individual can be changed and a new ordering of society achieved – a hope shared by many nourished in liberal and humanistic values, who find it hard to identify with a traditional religious community. Indeed, religions' own record is chequered, but their message of hope, based not on an easy optimism, but on confidence in a transcendent or spiritual dimension to life, can still inspire ordinary people to resist the downward spiral of violence and to work for a more just and peaceful world.

Religion often fuels the fire of violence and terrorism. It can reinforce and sanctify communal division and can give to the defeated terrorist a martyr's crown. In Northern Ireland, the Middle East, Sri Lanka, the Punjab and elsewhere, religious differences complicate other causes of division and can make opposing factions believe they are defending a holy cause – even if their religious leaders reject such claims.

Those of Asian origin in Britain may feel that discrimination against them is not only a matter of colour and culture, but also creed. National occasions are still usually only Christian in character, although the Observance for Commonwealth Day at Westminster Abbey is multi-faith in character. Only slowly are school assemblies responding to the multi-faith composition of many schools. 'White' and 'Christian' are subtly combined in assumptions of superiority, so that even 'Black-led' church members often feel alienated from society and from other Christians. The media image of Islam or at times of Israel can create a negative image of Muslims or Jews in Britain, although they should no more be identified with Ayatollah Khomeine or Rabbi Kahane, than Christians with the Revd Ian Paisley. It seems too that church members often reflect the racist attitudes prevalent in society.

Yet increasingly religious people recognise that at root the modern crisis is spiritual and any answer must draw upon the resources of all the great faiths. Many people, it seems, have a sense of alienation, without close bonds with family or community, without a deep meaning and purpose to their lives and are unsure of moral values. There is ample evidence of a decline in institutional religion in this country. Those groups which do recruit a number of young people tend to be authoritarian or doctrinally conservative, for example, the House Church Movement or the new religious movements, perhaps springing from Asia or California.

Complaints about a retreating age of faith or a decline in morals are nothing new and as 'Live Aid' and 'Sport Aid' have shown, there is a deep reservoir of compassion that may be tapped. Yet how deep down does this concern for others go? Violence on the picket line or in demonstrations, wanton attacks on the elderly or young women show a disregard for humanistic values. The cruelty of the terrorist in sending innocent people to their deaths is a denial of our common humanity. The terrible acts of genocide in Uganda, Kampochea and, peculiarly horrible, the Holocaust, provoke disturbing questions about the evil that lurks within. It is too easy to condemn some war criminals without examining our own potential for bestial cruelty. It was mostly ordinary people who drove the trains to the death camps and who guarded the inmates. What are the pressures that, in many countries, turn people into torturers? Irving Greenberg[1] has spoken of a moral vacuum and the breakdown of the secular absolute. Some commentators, for example, seem to excuse terrorists' atrocities because of sympathy for their cause and the injustices suffered by those for whom they campaign. But no cause should make terrorist acts morally acceptable. We lack the deep commitment to humanistic and moral values which would make torture and genocide unthinkable and the release of nuclear warheads inconceivable.

Increasingly it is being seen that the restatement of shared moral values is the common calling of members of the great faiths and all people of goodwill. Lord Sorensen, who was Chairman of the World Congress of Faiths in the 1960s, held that in the world religions there could be found an essential moral content transcending communal codes. Aware of the great variety of moral patterns or *mores*, Lord Sorensen said: 'It is necessary to distinguish between paramount moral values and what I term "moral patterns" '.[2] Among the moral values to be found in all religions, he claimed, are justice, mercy, compassion, integrity, courage, sacrifice, fidelity and fraternity. Others have pointed to the existence of 'The Golden Rule' in some form in almost all religious traditions. Sir Francis Younghusband himself, who founded the Congress fifty years ago, hoped that the fellowship of faiths would encourage a world loyalty and a deepening compassion in which people sensed their oneness with others. Writing soon after the outbreak of the Second World War, he said,

> A new world order is now the dream of men, but for this a new spirit will be needed. This is the special concern of men of religion, in this case of all religions . . . all combined to create a world loyalty and a sense of world fellowship and to provide the spiritual impetus, the dynamic and the direction to the statesmen and economists, whose business it is to give it bodily expression.[3]

In a similar way, part of the purpose of the Council of Christians and Jews – founded in the 1940s – was to promote the fundamental ethical teachings which are common to both religions and to bring together Jews and Christians to fight all forms of prejudice, intolerance and discrimination.

More recently the World Conference on Religion and Peace has brought together representatives of most major faith communities in an on-going concern for peace and justice. As the former Secretary General, Dr Homer Jack, said after the first

Assembly in Kyoto, 'We have learned, in using our religious and ethical insights, to leap over theology and discuss the next steps for human survival, which tend to parallel the agenda of the United Nations'.[4] In 1984, a United Nations Interfaith Colloquium against Apartheid was held in London, chaired by Bishop Trevor Huddleston. At the Vancouver Assembly of the World Council of Churches, the commitment of Christians to work with others for peace, justice and human rights was affirmed and the same call has been made on more than one occasion by the Pope, for example during his pastoral visit to India in 1986. A similar commitment has been voiced by leaders of other great religions, such as Dr Niwano of Rissho Kosei-Kai of Japan or at the 1986 International Interfaith Seminar on National Integration and Human Solidarity, held at Madras Christian College, India.

Yet whilst it is important that religious leaders should speak together about shared moral values, it is harder to see what religious people can in fact do to change the climate of violence and division. First, perhaps, there is the continuing task of overcoming prejudice. Too often members of one community have a false stereotyped view of those of other faiths. Increasingly, for example, Christians are recognising that their picture of Judaism is distorted. At its worst, Christians have regarded the Jews as guilty of deicide and diabolised them. It is now recognised that Jesus was killed by the Roman authorities. Even if some Jews wanted him out of the way, it is morally wrong to hold all Jews then or subsequently collectively responsible. Such false teaching has been repudiated by the Churches, but only after it had contributed to the terrible suffering of many Jews. Still, many Christians wrongly think of Judaism as a legalistic religion and assume that they have replaced the Jews as the people of God. The exclusive views of some Christians who claim to have a monopoly of salvation also underlie attitudes of superiority towards others and even the hidden racism of some Christians.

Slowly Muslim scholars are recognising that the initial Muslim reaction to Hinduism as 'idolatry' was superficial.[5] The various representations of the divine in Hinduism point to one Divine Reality. The ancient and orthodox writer, Raghunandana, wrote, for example, that it was for the sake of the devotee that 'we fancy forms and shapes of that Brahman which is pure spirit, the

One without a second, the absolutely simple and incorporeal One.'[6] Yet still people in the West speak of Hindus as polytheists. I recall too my surprise on first meeting a priest of one of the great Shinto shrines of Japan. I had thought of it as a rather nationalist and limited religion, but the priest spoke elegantly of his faith's central message of the unity of all people as children of the One Heavenly Father. I was privileged later to be invited to share in a Shinto ceremony.

There is a continuing task to help people to a proper and respectful awareness of the beliefs and practices of others. Too often we have born 'false witness' against them. It is now an accepted principle of inter-religious dialogue that people should be allowed to define their faith for themselves, rather than be fitted into other people's categories. Even in the nineteenth century the Anglican theologian F.D. Maurice said man will not be really intelligible to us, if instead of listening to him, we determine to classify him.

Even more important is encouraging members of one community to meet those of another. As personal friendships develop, stereotypes dissolve. At the Corrymeela community in Northern Ireland, courses are arranged for young Protestants and young Roman Catholics to spend time together. At the end of one such week, a Protestant was heard to say of a Catholic, 'he's not all bad'. In Israel, Neve Shalom, at its School for Peace, brings together young Arabs and Jews. One young Jewish participant in a workshop there wrote afterwards to his Arab counsellor, 'Now, when I hear of demonstrations or strikes, I consider carefully the stark facts from a different angle and try to understand the motivation behind the action and the emotions which produce such events'.[7] There are many attempts to foster such understanding, from the United World Colleges or the United Nations University for Peace to school exchanges and the twinning of towns. It is a slow business, because there is no substitute for the personal experience of real encounter with those from other cultural backgrounds.

Even so, it is difficult on return to avoid the pressures to conform to the stereotyped images of others that are dominant in the society to which we belong. This is why those who take part in interfaith dialogue often feel marginalized in their own community. There is need for a radical change in the appreciation religions have of each other. Long ago, the Buddhist Emperor Asoka said, 'The faiths of others all deserve to be honoured – by honouring them one exalts one's own faith and at the same time performs a service to the faiths of others'.[8]

Yet for those religions that make exclusive claims to know God's truth, it is hard to avoid devaluing the faiths of others. The Asian Christian Choan-Seng Song speaks of 'centrism', in which 'my likes and dislikes become normative' and in which 'we cannot see virtues in those who differ from us'. Centrism, he says, 'makes us blind to how God is at work in persons of all sorts and conditions'.[9] He goes on to suggest that Christian centrism – the assumption that the Christian experience of God is normative – has led Christians to devalue women, blacks and those of other cultures and faiths. In Judaism too, the consciousness of being a chosen people can, wrongly, be understood in an exclusive superior way and the same temptation exists in other faith communities – even the tolerance of modern Hinduism is on its own terms and presuppositions.

Yet an easy relativism does not satisfy the believer. The life of worship and devotion demand an absoluteness. If we do not give ourselves to the One who is most holy, it is idolatry. Commitment is to the Truth. The challenge to religious people today is to be at once deeply committed and radically open to others. This is possible if, whilst we surrender ourselves in worship, we recognise that our perception of the One adored falls far short of his glory – 'we see through a glass darkly, not yet face to face'. Our commitment is to the truth that we perceive, but that truth is always open to correction and enlargement. 'God is most great.' God is always greater than our understanding. The constant danger is of putting our religion in the place of God and so making of it an idol, which is the failing of the fanatic. There is in most faiths an apophatic or mystical tradition, which reminds us that the Divine Mystery transcends our understanding. 'Neti, neti', says the Hindu, whilst the Buddha dismissed metaphysical speculation and the Christian father, St Gregory of Nazianzen (329–389), spoke of God as 'beyond all name'.

Recognising the limitations of our understanding, it is possible to discern a positive value in religious differences. There are profound differences of belief between the great religions as well as areas of agreement. These differences may in part be a God-given check on our human tendency to religious pride. Perhaps, however, they are also complementary or convergent, suggesting that no one tradition can fully comprehend the mystery of God, just as in a family each member has a different appreciation of other members of the family, yet together they give a complete picture. The American R.E. Whitson has spoken of each religion being both 'unique' and 'universal'. Unique in that it springs from a distinct central or core experience, but universal in that its meaning is relevant to all people. As Bishop George Appleton, former Anglican Archbishop in Jerusalem, said in a sermon to mark the 40th anniversary of the World Congress of Faiths,

> Each religion has a message, a gospel, a central affirmation. Each of us needs to enlarge on the gospel which he has received without wanting to demolish the gospel of others . . . We can enlarge and deepen our initial and basic faith by the experience and insights of people from other religions and cultures without disloyalty to our own commitment.[10]

This suggests an approach of mutual witness and sharing, where people of different faiths meet in a spirit of friendship and understanding to share with others their apprehension of God. This is in contrast to the missionary approach, which can seem a form of spiritual aggression. Believers have too often interpreted their claims to uniqueness, truth and chosenness in a way that fuels the divisions in our society and may aggravate communal strife and violence. Certainly not all that passes as religion is healthy and critical faculties are needed as much here as elsewhere. The discernment required is between true and false *religion* rather than between true and false *religions*. How is it that religion may release life-giving compassion rather than devour a person in a negativity that is destructive of them and of others?

The essential call of each religion is to inner transformation. Violence, whatever its social, political and economic causes, springs from inner division and aggression. Whilst some religious traditions sanction the use of force to restrain violence and aggression, none believe that sin and evil can be overcome in this way. As Jesus said, 'Out of a man's heart come evil thoughts, acts of fornication, of theft, murder, adultery, ruthless greed and malice'.[11] The Buddha taught, 'Victory brings hate, because the defeated man is unhappy. He who renounces victory and defeat, this man finds joy. For hate is not conquered by hate: hate is conquered by love. This is a law eternal'.[12] The United Nations Charter also says, 'It is in the minds of men that wars begin'. Rightly therefore, the universal prayer for peace begins with the personal, before it leads into prayer for the world:

> Lead me from Death to Life
> From Falsehood to Truth,
> Lead me from Despair to Hope
> From Fear to Trust
> Lead me from Hate to Love
> From War to Peace
> Let Peace fill our Hearts,
> Our World, our Universe.

The inner transformation for which the religions call allows little by little our natural aggression to be sublimated; it integrates the person, healing guilt and bitterness. It brings an inner peace by opening our individual being to the Divine Reality in whom is wholeness, peace and unity. Prayer or contemplation and meditation and religious rituals renew the individual's contact with the Spiritual Source of Life. It is significant that a worker with drug addicts could say that the only real recoveries he has known are with those who discover a spiritual basis to their lives. Perhaps also the only healing for those caught up in violence and terrorism is the discovery of meaning and wholeness in a religious faith.

Such inner change is needed in each of us individually. This central call of the religions is misunderstood by those in public life who expect religions to reinforce the moral order. Most clergy will have had the experience of visiting a school and finding themselves used as one more means of imposing discipline by a desperate teacher. 'What will the vicar think', wails the helpless teacher to her noisy class. There was a time when the religious leaders shared in the authority structures of British society. Even amongst the faithful, the number whose behaviour is dictated by what the Bible or Church tells them is decreasing. Moral behaviour is interiorised. People, educated maybe by the Bible and the Church, act according to what they in themselves believe to be right or God's will. In some Islamic states, religion is used to reinforce an externally imposed pattern of moral behaviour, but to hope that religion could be used in such a way in a democratic society would be a denial of liberal values and, in my view, a perversion of religion.

Such an emphasis on inner change may seem an inadequate response to violence and disorder in our society and across the world. Clearly, as I have suggested above, religions do have a social responsibility, especially to uphold moral and humanistic values. Religious people are caught up with others in the struggle for social justice. Yet if religious bodies seem too political or too institutional, they alienate people and hide from them the essential inner quest. There is no short cut, because only the person who has begun to find inner liberation can help to liberate others.

It is significant therefore that some of those who in this century have been most effective in achieving social change have had a deep religious motivation, such as Mahatma Gandhi, Martin Luther King, Archbishop Helder Camara and many others. Thomas Merton, one of the twentieth century masters of contemplation, was led by his contemplation to political involvement. In his *Contemplative Prayer*,[13] he argued that

> this is an age that by its very nature as a time of crisis, of revolution, of struggle, calls for the special searching and questioning which are the work of the monk in meditation and prayer . . . In reality the monk abandons the world in order to listen more intently to the deepest and most neglected voices that proceed from its inner depths.

In silence and withdrawal, the contemplative perceives the real values and issues at stake in the world and is compelled to challenge false gods. Fr. Alfred Delp, a Jesuit who was imprisoned in Nazi Germany, believed that solitude was a vital prerequisite for the awakening of the social conscience. 'Great issues affecting mankind', he wrote, 'have to be decided in the wilderness, in uninterrupted isolation and unbroken silence.'[14] 'In solitude, in the depths of man's own aloneness, lie the resources for resistance to injustice',[15] wrote Thomas Merton, and the American peaceworker Daniel Berrigan said, 'The time will shortly be upon us . . . when the pursuit of contemplation becomes a strictly subversive activity'.[16]

The withdrawal of the contemplative is not therefore withdrawal from the world, but for the world. This is perhaps a distinctive feature of the spirituality of the twentieth century and is not confined to one religious tradition. Whilst religions say that real change requires internal transformation, that transformation is expressed in participation in the struggle for social justice and in political action. At the end of the last century, the Hindu reformer, Swami Vivekananda, at Kanyakumari, on what is now called Vivekananda rock, dedicated himself to the service of 'My God, the wicked; My God, the afflicted, My God, the poor of all races'. 'At Cape Comorin', he wrote later from America,

> I hit upon a plan. We are so many sannyasins wandering about and teaching the people metaphysics – it is all madness. Did not our Gurudeva use to say 'An empty stomach is no use for religion'? Suppose some disinterested sannyasins, bent on doing good to others, go from village to village disseminating education and seeking in various ways to better the condition of all down to the *chandala* [a man of lowest caste] . . . can't that bring forth good in time?[17]

Indeed the Ramakrishna Mission has become one of the most active Hindu organisations for educational work and social reform. Mahatma Gandhi also taught that

> the only way to find God is to see him in his creation and to be one with it. This can only be done by the service of all, *sarvodaya*. I am part and parcel of the whole and I cannot find Him apart from the rest of humanity . . . If I could persuade myself that I could find Him in a Himalayan cave, I would proceed there immediately. But I know that I cannot find Him apart from humanity.[18]

In Vietnam, the Buddhist monks became active in the search for peace and Buddhists have shown recently increasing social concern. For some Jews, Israel presents the opportunity to fashion a society obedient to God's will. The World Council of Churches has attracted bitter criticism because of the radical stance it has adopted on many current issues, especially racism. Christians have been in the forefront of the struggle against Apartheid in South Africa, whilst in Latin America, the struggle against economic and political oppression has inspired Liberation Theology.

Opponents accuse religious leaders of dabbling in politics. They may lack political or economic expertise and not all are free from self-deception. Yet the authentic spiritual leaders of our age are compelled to involvement by their apprehension of God and of His purposes for the world. Usually, whilst they recognise injustice as a cause of violence, they reject violence as its cure. Their faith nourishes the hope that real improvement is possible and they trust that the final outcome is in the hands of God, whose purposes are good. This faith can save them from the revolutionary's impatience which leads to violence. To sustain hope is perhaps the greatest contribution religious people can make. During the Second World War, the artist Naum Gabo was asked how he could justify spending time on his visionary constructions, which seemed so remote from the agonies of war. 'A world at war', he replied,

> it seems to me, may have the right to reject my work as irrelevant to its immediate needs. I can say but little in my defence. I can only beg to be believed that I suffer with all the world in all the misfortunes which are fallen upon us. I try to guard in my work the image of the morrow we left behind us in our memories and foregone aspirations, and to remind us that the image of the world can be different.[19]

Religions too point to the 'image of a world that is different' and inspire their followers to struggle towards that vision. The Messianic hope has been taken over into Christianity, with the dream of a new heaven and a new earth. Although at times Christians have focused on the next world, they have through the centuries prayed that God's kingdom would come on earth as it is in heaven. Hindus with their cyclic view of history have not always given meaning to the historical process. Yet a modern writer such as Sri Aurobindo has suggested that the meaning of

166 The Violent Society

evolution is for man to grow in consciousness till he reaches complete and perfect consciousness, not only in his individual, but in his collective, that is to say, social life. The Saiva Siddhantin scholar Dr Devasenapathi said in his Miller lectures at Madras, 'From a savage to a saint, isn't that a perfect description of the increasing purpose in all history and the meaning of it all'.[20]

In each religion, the details of the hope for the future of humankind are varied and uncertain, but in them all there is the confidence that violence, terror and disorder can, under God, be overcome by self-sacrifice and compassion. This, as Gandhi made clear, is not a weak compromise with evil. Gandhi held that *ahimsa* (usually translated as non-violence) is a technique of resistance to injustice that does not lead to a vicious circle of spiralling violence. It is a method of struggle to build the contours of a peaceful society.

Beyond the immediate political, social and economic steps necessary to check violence, religious people, if they overcome their prejudicial attitudes to each other, can affirm together shared moral and humanistic values, point people to the inner transformation that liberates from aggression, and inspire a hope which renews those who struggle against forces of division and destruction. All this, because their faith is rooted in a transcendent or spiritual order.

Solzhenitsyn, in *The Gulag Archipelago*, tells of a non-political offender, who declared a lengthy hunger strike. The Prosecutor went to his cell and asked him, 'Why are you torturing yourself?' The man replied, 'Justice is more precious to me than life'. This so astonished his prosecutor with its irrelevance that he had the man at once transferred to an asylum. I myself remember visiting a concentration camp cell, used for solitary confinement, where on the blue plaster, an unknown prisoner had etched with his thumbnail a picture of *Christus Victor* – the Lord who overcomes every evil.

Such confidence can offer us the hope that society's ills are not insoluble and give us the patience to treat the violent with compassion.

## NOTES

1. Irving Greenberg, 'Cloud of Smoke, Pillar of Fire, Judaism, Christianity and Modernity after the Holocaust', in *Auschwitz, Beginning of a New Era? Reflections on the Holocaust*, ed. Eva Fleischner, Ktav, 1977, p. 29.
2. Reginald Sorensen, World Congress of Faiths Conference Sermon in *World Faiths*, No. 77, Autumn 1969, p. 19. See also his book *I Believe in Man*, Lindsey Press, 1970.
3. Quoted in A. Peacock's *Fellowship Through Religion*, World Congress of Faiths, London, 1956, p. 21.
4. *Religion for Peace*, Newsletter of the World Conference on Religion and Peace, July 1975, p. 2.
5. Zaki Badawi, 'Islam and World Religions' in *World Faiths Insight*, New Series 13, June 1986, p. 9.
6. Quoted by Fr. P. Fallon in *Religious Hinduism*, St Paul Publications, Allahabad, 1968, p. 75.
7. Neve Shalom School for Peace, Israel. Cyclostyled report on the Introductory Workshops, 1983. See also 'Bridgehead built for peace', *The Times*, 29 July 1986 (by Ian Murray).
8. Rock Edict XII, *Edicts of Asoka*, trans. N.A. Nikam and Richard McKeen, University of Chicago Press, Chicago 1959, p. 51.
9. Choan-Seng Song, *The Compassionate God. An Exercise in the Theology of Transposition*, SCM Press 1982, p. 132.
10. George Appleton, 'Faiths in Fellowship', *World Faiths*, No. 101, Spring 1977, pp. 4–5.
11. Mark 7, 21.
12. From the Dhammapada.
13. Thomas Merton, *Contemplative Prayer*, Darton, Longman and Todd, 1973, p. 25.
14. *The Prison Meditations of Father Alfred Delp*, Herder & Herder, New York, 1963, p. 95.
15. Quoted by Kenneth Leech, *The Social God*, Sheldon, 1981, p. 42.
16. Daniel Berrigan, *America is Hard to Find*, SPCK, 1973, pp. 77–8.
17. Quoted by D.S. Sarma, *Hinduism Through the Ages*, Bharatiya Vidya Bhavan, Bombay, p. 64.
18. Quoted from *Harijan* by Bede Griffiths in *Christian Ashram*, Darton, Longman and Todd, 1966, p. 127.
19. Quoted in *The Image of Life* by Brenda Lealman and Edward Robinson, Christian Education Movement, 1980, p. 9.
20. Devasenapathi, *Towards the Conquest of Time*. Madras, 1962, p. 39. See my *Together to the Truth*, Christian Literature Society, Madras, 1971, pp. 136–7.

# NOTES ON CONTRIBUTORS

Eric Moonman is Director of the Centre for Contemporary Studies and a former Member of Parliament. He is the author of several books including *The Alternative Government*.

The Rev. Marcus Braybrooke is the Executive Director of the Council of Christians and Jews. Since 1979 he has been the Director of Training in the Diocese of Bath and Wells. He is the editor of *World Faiths Insight*. He was formerly the Chairman of the Executive Committee of the World Congress of Faiths.

Richard Clutterbuck has been a lecturer in law at the University of Sussex in the School of Social Studies since 1977. His most recent writings are on Government and Law and Civil Liberties.

Jane Moonman is a magistrate and a trustee of the Basildon Emergency Accommodation Project. She is the Director of a public relations organisation.

Jim Patten is a member of the Council of the British Psychological Society and Honorary Secretary of the Society's Clinical Division. He is the principal Clinical Psychologist at Purdysburn Hospital, Belfast where his work involves him in therapy with victims of violence.

Geoffrey Pearson is Professor of Social Work at Middlesex Polytechnic. He is the author of *The Deviant Imagination, Working Class Youth Culture* and *Hooligan: A History of Respectable Fear*.

Paul Wilkinson is Professor of International Relations at the University of Aberdeen. His books include *The New Fascists*. He is a member of the Advisory Council of the Centre for Contemporary Studies.